GEOG 1HA3

Human Geographies: Society and Culture

Dr. Michael Mercier

COURSE HANDBOOK

2015-16 Term 2 (Winter)

SCHOOL OF GEOGRAPHY AND EARTH SCIENCES

McMaster University

Table of Contents

Preamble

Purpose of this Manual

This manual has been designed and written as a reference resource for students in the Introductory-level Human Geography courses, and is meant to be kept as a key reference guide for those in the B.A Geography programs to use throughout their studies. It includes guidelines for the development of important skills and concepts for use in the Human Geography courses, and for courses outside of the School of Geography & Earth Sciences (SGES). Students are strongly encouraged to keep this handbook and use it as a handy reference source.

We hope you find this manual useful in your studies and would appreciate any feedback on how we can improve future versions.

Geography and Earth Sciences at McMaster

At McMaster, the School of Geography & Earth Sciences is uniquely placed because it offers a variety of undergraduate programs leading to either a B.A. or B.Sc. degree (either Honours or three-year programs). Programs can focus on topics ranging from urban geography (the study of human activities in cities) to population and health geography (the study of spatial patterns of human health and disease), and from climatology (the study of the Earth's climate) to environmental science/studies, to name only a few. Below is a diagram which outlines these major pathways to undergraduate degrees from SGES:

ACADEMIC PROGRAMS

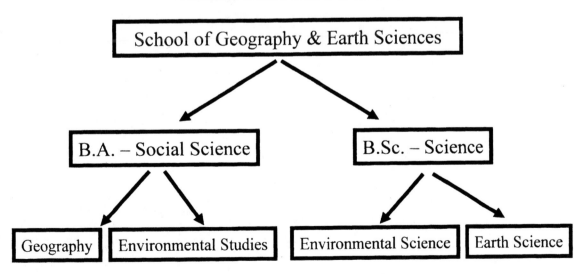

Level I - Human Geography/Environmental Studies & Earth Science/Environmental Science

At present, the School of Geography & Earth Sciences offers <u>four</u> Level I courses; two human geography/environmental studies courses, and two earth/environmental science courses.

Students interested in human geography (i.e. cities; the linkages between health and the environment; globalization; geopolitics; social and cultural diversity; economic development; transportation issues; maps and Geographic Information Systems (GIS), etc.) and/or a social scientific approach to environmental problems (environmental *studies*) should consider taking one or both of the Level I Human Geography/Environmental Studies courses. Typically, we offer both of these courses in both semesters of the traditional academic year, and both are usually offered in the summer as well.

Level I Human Geography/Environmental Studies courses offered by SGES:
- Human Geographies: Society & Culture (GEOG 1HA3)
- Human Geographies: City & Economy (GEOG 1HB3)

Students interested in aspects of the physical environment (i.e. climate; water issues and processes; geology and mining; soil science; contaminant remediation; air and water pollution; climate change, etc.) should consider taking one or both of the Level I Earth Science/Environmental Science courses. These courses are the springboard to the B.Sc. degrees offered by the School of Geography & Earth Sciences. Typically, these courses are offered twice per academic year, and occasionally in the summer as well.

Level I Earth Science/Environmental Science courses offered by SGES:
- Earth and the Environment (EARTH SC 1GO3/ENVIR SC 1GO3)
- Climate, Water and the Environment (ENVIR SC 1CO3)

Programs - Human Geography/Environmental Studies at McMaster: Beyond Level I

Students interested in pursuing a program in Human Geography or Environmental Studies have four programs that they can choose from:

- Honours B.A. in Geography
- Honours B.A. in Geography & Environmental Studies
- Combined Honours B.A. in Geography & Another Subject (from within the Faculties of Social Science or Humanities)
- B.A. in Geography

Key information about these programs, such as admissions requirements, course requirements, and elective opportunities can be obtained from the Undergraduate Calendar (available in print or online from the Office of the Registrar) or from the School of Geography & Earth Sciences website:

- http://www.science.mcmaster.ca/~geo/
    - o Search under 'undergraduate studies/programs'

If you are interested in, or have any questions about, registering in (or transferring into) the B.A. programs in Geography, Geography & Environmental Studies, or a combined program between Geography and another discipline (e.g. Sociology, History, etc.), please feel free to contact one of the following members of the School of Geography & Earth Sciences (SGES) who would be happy to provide further guidance to you:

- Kara Salvador – Academic (Undergraduate) Program Advisor
    - o Email: ugadmin@mcmaster.ca   Phone: ext. 20122   Office: GSB 218

- Michael Mercier – B.A. Program Advisor and Level I Geography Professor
    - o Email: mercieme@mcmaster.ca   Phone: ext. 27597   Office: GSB 220

- B.A. Program Advising (Geography / Environmental Studies): sgesba@mcmaster.ca
- B.Sc. Program Advising (Earth Science / Environmental Science): sgesbsc@mcmaster.ca

The School of Geography & Earth Science main office is located in the General Science Building (GSB). The main office is GSB 206.
- SGES Website: http: www.science.mcmaster.ca/geo

Courses - Human Geography/Environmental Studies at McMaster: Beyond Level I

The two introductory-level human geography courses (GEOG 1IIA3 & GEOG 1HB3) act as the stepping stones to human geography and environmental studies course offerings in SGES at Levels II-IV. Recent restructuring of the B.A. programs in Geography and Geography & Environmental Studies has resulted in an exciting new framework for our courses, and the addition of many brand-new courses. The chart below shows how these revisions have led to a new thematic organization of our courses.

Human Geography & Environmental Studies: Thematic Course Organization

Years II-IV

Urban: Social, Cultural & Economic Dimensions of Cities

The Environment: Issues, Policy, Planning, Resources, etc.

Health & Population: Health, Health-Care, Aging, etc.

Economy: Local/Global Issues, Transportation Analysis, etc.

GIS: Geographic Information Systems – Theory & Applied

Topics: Globalization, Geopolitics, Social/Cultural Geography

Regional: World, Canada, United States, Brazil, Africa, etc.

Core: Research Methods, Field Studies & Statistical Analysis

Fundamentally, the B.A. program course offerings at Levels II-IV have been organized around the following major subfields or themes:

- Urban Studies
- The Environment
- Health & Population
- Economic Geography
- Geographical Information Systems (GIS)

Each of these themes has an 'introductory' course at Level II, along with a series of more specialized and topical courses at both Level III and IV (***see diagram below***). Students are in no way limited to taking courses only from within one or two of these themes. In fact, program students can take as many of the Level II 'introductory' theme courses as they like, which then opens the possibility of taking any number of the Level III and IV courses within those themes.

In addition to these themes of courses, there are a series of 'core' courses where key concepts in research methods, field study, and critical analysis and writing, and so on are provided.

And finally, there are a series of general interest geography courses which have been organized into either 'regional geography' or 'topics in human geography' theme areas. The regional geography courses allow students to explore a variety of aspects of the geography (human and physical) of interesting places around the world (i.e., Canada, United States, Brazil, Europe, Italy, South-east Asia, India, Japan, Africa, etc.). Similarly, the topics in human geography courses allow students to further develop their interests in some of the key topical areas of the discipline, such as globalization, geopolitics, social geography and cultural geography.

COURSE CHART: Geography & Environmental Studies (BA & BA HONS)

Level I	Core							
	Society & Culture City & Economy							

Level II	Core	GIS	Environment	Health & Population	Urban	Economy	Topics in Human Geography	Regional Geography
		Geographic Information Systems	Environmental Issues	Geographies of Death & Disease	Cities in a Changing World	Economic Geography	Society and Space Landscapes and Culture	World Regional Geography Canada United States Mapping our World

Level III	Core	GIS	Environment	Health & Population	Urban	Economy	Topics in Human Geography	Regional Geography
	Research Methods in Human Geography Statistical Analysis Field Camp (E.S.) Field Camp (H.G.) Service Learning Internship Geography Internship	Advanced Raster GIS Advanced Vector GIS Remote Sensing	Energy & Society Sustainability and the Economy Environmental Catastrophes	Population Growth & Aging Geography of Health & Health-Care	Urban Historical Geography Urban Social Geography Planning Our Cities Cities of the Developing World	Transportation Geography Locational Analysis	Power, Politics and Space Geographies of Globalization	Regional Geography of a Selected World Region I Regional Geography of a Selected World Region II

Level IV	Core	GIS	Environment	Health & Population	Urban	Economy	Topics in Human Geography	Regional Geography
	Independent Study Senior Thesis Senior Field Camp	Applied Spatial Statistics Special Topics in GIS GIS Programming	Environmental Assessment Environmental Policy, Ethics & Risk	Geographies of Disability Public & Community Health Environment & Health	Urban Places, Urban Dreams Urban Housing	Transport Policy Transportation Systems Analysis Geographies of the North American Political Economy	Geography of Gender Special Topics in Human Geography	

1.0   Course Guide: Course Information & Policies

1.1   Introduction: Overview & Sessional/Course Dates

This handbook contains the following important materials:

- Course Outline (Chapter 1)
- Important Course Information & Policies (Chapter 1)
- Tutorial Materials & Exercises (Chapter 2)
- Assignments (Chapter 2)
- Handbook for Geography & Environmental Studies Students (Chapters 3-8)

Sessional and Course Dates: *Term 2 (Winter) 2015-16*

January 5:	Classes Begin
January 13:	Last Day to Drop/Add Courses
Week of January 18-22:	**Tutorials Begin**
February 6:	**Mid-Term Examination**
February 15-19:	No Classes or Tutorials – Reading Break
February 15:	*Family Day Holiday*
March 25:	*Good Friday Holiday*
Week of March 28-April 1:	**Tutorials Finish**
April 8:	Last Day of Classes
April 12-29:	Examination Period

1.2   Course Outline and Lecture Schedule

SESSION:	Winter 2016 – January 5 to April 29, 2016	
INSTRUCTOR:	Dr. Michael Mercier Office: GSB – 220 Phone: ext. 27597 Email: mercieme@mcmaster.ca	
CLASS HOURS:	Wednesday 9:30 AM - 10:20 AM Friday 9:30 AM - 10:20 AM	Location: MDCL 1305 Location: MDCL 1305
OFFICE HOURS:	Tuesday 2:30 PM – 4:20 PM Wednesday 10:30 AM – 12:20 PM	Location: GSB 220 Location: GSB 220

INTRODUCTION:
This outline contains important information regarding course structure, nature of instruction, forms of evaluation, and content of the course. More detailed information about these matters, as well as all course policies, can be found in the custom courseware (listed below). The Instructor and the TAs will review these materials in the first lecture and first tutorial.

COURSE DESCRIPTION:
Geography is concerned with the study of patterns and processes on the earth's surface. One branch of the discipline, human geography, focuses on the spatial organization of people, their cultures, economies, settlements, political and social structures, and behaviour. In other words, human geography is the study of the spatial organization of human activities and the meanings attached to the places where activities take place. Human geographic inquiry extends from the scale of the individual to that of the entire world.

At McMaster, students are introduced to human geography via two 3-unit Level I courses: GEOG 1HA3 & GEOG 1HB3. These two courses are related to one another (in the sense that they introduce students to the discipline of human geography), but are designed to be independent of each other. This means, students can take either course, or both courses (either simultaneously or consecutively), and still get a general understanding of what human geography is all about. *Students interested in a Geography or Environmental Studies program are encouraged to take both courses.*

The purpose of <u>this</u> course is to provide an introduction to the theories, methods, and patterns of human geography, and in particular ***social and cultural geography***. This course offers a geographic perspective on social and cultural phenomena. Topics include: the significance of culture and cultural difference (including language, ethnicity, race, gender, and religion); cities as forms of cultural settlements, and the rise of urban societies; the meanings of cultural landscapes; the importance of geographical perspectives in global politics; and the relationship between the environment and health. The course is an overview of the field and acts as a foundation for: (i) subsequent human geography courses offered by the School; and (ii) for general global understanding and awareness.

By the end of the course students should be able to: (1) identify and define the main geographical concepts related to the study of human activity; (2) select appropriate concepts and apply them to specific geographic problems; and (3) communicate ideas clearly and concisely in both verbal and written form.

INSTRUCTION:
This course has both lecture and tutorial components. Each week, students are to attend two one-hour lectures. Lectures will be designed around the discussion of core material. Tutorials will meet most weeks of the term for approximately two hours. The tutorials will be used to present material essential for the course assignments as well as to develop essential skills and to discuss course materials in small groups and collaboratively. Attendance in both lectures and tutorials is expected. This course has an Avenue to Learn ('A2L' or 'Avenue') site, and materials will be deposited there regularly; you are encouraged to make use of this technology daily.

READING MATERIAL:
Text: Norton, W. 2013. <u>Human Geography</u> (8th Edition). Toronto, Ont.: Oxford University Press. (**Required**)
Custom Courseware: GEOG 1HA3 - Human Geographies: Society & Culture (Winter 2016). (**Required**)

EVALUATION & GRADING:
For this course you will be evaluated on the basis of two written assignments and two written examinations covering material addressed in lectures, tutorials and readings. The assignments are designed to engage you in important human geography

concepts, but almost as importantly to help you develop important skills in written communication and synthesis; some group work will be required. The assignments are designed to help you to draw connections between concepts discussed in lectures and readings and real world geographic examples. Details about the assignments will be provided through the tutorials at a later date.

Mid Term Exam	Date: ***Saturday February 6th (10:30 AM – 12:00 PM)***	15%
Assignments & Tutorials	Dates: Various Dates throughout Term	45%
• *Assignment 1 (7 %); Assignment 2 (20 %); Tutorials and Participation (18 %)*		
Final Exam	Date: April Exam Period	40%

TENTATIVE LECTURE SCHEDULE: Topics & Readings (subject to change)

Date:	Section:	Topic	Readings
Jan. 6	**Introduction**	Introduction & Course Overview: What is Geography?	Intro. & Ch.1
Jan. 8		Key Concepts in Human Geography I	Ch.2
Jan. 13		Key Concepts in Human Geography II	Ch.2
Jan. 15		Geographic Tools: The Map – Social & Cultural Interpretations	Ch.2
Jan. 20	**Population & Health Geographies**	Global Population - The Big Picture	Ch.5
Jan. 22		Social & Cultural Determinants of Population Change	Ch.5
Jan. 27		Theories & Consequences of Population Change	Ch.5
Jan. 29		Geographies of Health & Health-Care	
Feb. 3	**Social & Cultural Geographies**	The Geography of Culture	Ch.7
Feb. 5		The Geography of Language	Ch.7
Feb. 10		The Geography of Religion	Ch.7
Feb. 12		The Geographies of Race & Ethnicity	Ch.8
Feb. 17	*No Class*	*No Class – Reading Week*	
Feb. 19	*No Class*	*No Class – Reading Week*	
Feb. 24		Cultural Landscapes & the Geographies of Popular Culture	Ch.8
Feb. 26	**Geographies of Cities & Settlement**	Introduction to Forms of Settlement: Rural Settlements	Ch.11
Mar. 2		Cities and Urban Forms of Settlement	Ch.11
Mar. 4		Urbanization and Urban Morphology	Ch.11
Mar. 9		Urban Social Geography	Ch.12 & Ch.13
Mar. 11		Urban History & Urban Landscapes – Reading the Urban Landscape	
Mar. 16		Social & Cultural Urban Issues	Ch.13
Mar. 18		G.I.S.: Social & Cultural Geographic Applications	Ch.2
Mar. 23	**Political Geographies**	Introduction to Political Geography: States, Nations & Territories	Ch.9
Mar. 25	*No Class*	*No Class – Good Friday*	
Mar. 30		Geopolitics & State Stability/Instability	Ch.9
Apr. 1		Geographies of War, Peace & Terrorism	Ch.9
Apr. 6		Electoral Geographies	Ch.9
Apr. 8	**Conclusion**	Human Geography: Overview and Prospects	Concl.

Accommodations for Students with Disabilities:
Students with disabilities may receive accommodations to assist them in the completion of their assignments and exams. Please contact Student Accessibility Services (MUSC Lower Level) and the Instructor as soon as possible if you require assistance.

Policy Regarding Academic Dishonesty:
You are expected to exhibit honesty and use ethical behaviour in all aspects of the learning process. Academic credentials you earn are rooted in principles of honesty and academic integrity.

Academic dishonesty is to knowingly act or fail to act in a way that results, or could result, in unearned academic credit or advantage. This behaviour can result in serious consequences, e.g. the grade of zero on an assignment, loss of credit with a notation on the transcript (notation reads: "Grade of F assigned for academic dishonesty"), and/or suspension or expulsion from the university.

It is your responsibility to understand what constitutes academic dishonesty. For information on the various types of academic dishonesty please refer to the Academic Integrity Policy, located at www.mcmaster.ca/academicintegrity

The following illustrates only three forms of academic dishonesty:
1. Plagiarism, e.g. the submission of work that is not one's own or for which other credit has been obtained.
2. Improper collaboration in group work.
3. Copying or using unauthorized aids in tests and examinations.

Please Note: The Instructor and University reserve the right to modify elements of the course during the term. The University may change the dates and deadlines for any or all courses in extreme circumstances. If either type of modification becomes necessary, reasonable notice and communication with the students will be given with explanation and the opportunity to comment on changes. It is the responsibility of the student to check their McMaster email and course websites weekly during the term and to note any changes.

1.3   *Guide to Lectures and Readings*

Learning at a university level involves a variety of different tools. In this course, you will be learning about human geography via lectures, textbook readings, individual and group assignments, and tutorial activities and discussions. In this section we provide you with some guidance on how to maximize your learning from two of these tools, the lecture and the textbook readings. Discussion about the assignments and tutorial components of the course will be outlined in subsequent sections of this manual.

1.3.1   *The University Lecture:*

Most students in Level I courses are not familiar with the lecture as a teaching method. High school classes tend to be very structured and highly interactive. Furthermore, students are usually told what to write in their notes. University lectures, on the other hand, place the onus on the student in terms of advance preparation, what ideas to include in the notes taken during the lecture and follow-up study. Lectures serve the following purposes:

1.   to present information
2.   to challenge students to think about the course material
3.   to establish links among the various components of the course

It should be stressed that lecturing styles vary considerably from one Instructor to another. This requires that students make the necessary adjustments (especially during lectures) so as to enhance their understanding of the material presented. The following ideas are intended to help make the lectures and textbook readings more meaningful components of this course for you.

1.3.2   *Lectures - Advance Preparation:*

The first step in making the lectures more worthwhile is advance preparation. Students can prepare for each class by: (1) consulting the course outline (to see where each lecture topic fits into the overall structure of the course); and (2) reading the relevant textbook materials (as listed in the lecture schedule portion of the course outline). By doing this prior to the lecture you will have at least some familiarity with the topic being discussed in class, thereby making the class more rewarding and giving you a clue as to the most important parts of the lecture.

1.3.3   *Lectures – Taking Notes During the Lecture:*

The most frequently asked questions about lectures concern what should be written in one's notes. **Do not be content to just write down only those things the Instructor writes on the board, overhead projector or Power Point slide – this information will never be sufficient for your later needs**. At the same time it is not necessary (nor is it possible) to write down everything the Instructor says. Between these two extremes is a happy medium which will vary from one student to the next. It takes time and practice to develop good note-taking habits. The following suggestions will help in developing these habits:

1.   Come to class prepared (see above)

2. Write down the main ideas and any other notes necessary to understand what is said
3. Make note of key examples provided by the lecturer to emphasize and illustrate key concepts; these examples will often provide the basis for good answers/responses to test/exam questions
4. Use short forms and/or symbols for frequently used words or phrases
5. All diagrams/graphs should be fully labelled and accompanied by explanatory notes
6. Pay attention to what the lecturer is saying; do not talk to others, do not spend class time sending emails, text messaging, or otherwise being distracted

1.3.4 Lectures – Reflection After the Lecture:

Finally, it is also essential to review your notes immediately after the class, while the concepts are still relatively fresh in your mind. In reviewing your notes you should aim to see how the lecture fits with the preceding lecture(s) as well as the reading(s) for that class. It is a good idea to make a set of summary notes containing definitions of important concepts as well as the main point(s) of the lecture. This summary will aid in your understanding the lecture material and will also serve as a useful study guide for tests and exams. Make a note of any questions you have and consult with your TA or Instructor as soon as possible. It is important to think critically about the information which is presented in lectures and readings, i.e., just because the Instructor says something doesn't mean that this is the way it is. Ask yourself if what has been said makes sense to you. Does it agree with what you already know and believe? Your university experience will be greatly enhanced by developing the ability to think critically and to ask questions about what you learn.

1.3.5 Textbook Reading:

Equally important to attending lectures, taking good notes during lectures, and reflecting about the lecture content afterwards, is reading the assigned textbook. Your Instructor will outline which sections of the book are relevant to the course (and the lecture schedule, which is part of the course outline, also indicates which sections of the book you need to read for each lecture).

A subject as broad as human geography cannot be adequately covered in a series of approximately 24 lectures (of 50 minutes each). As such, there is much that needs to be learned independently outside of the classroom via textbook readings. These readings in some cases will provide important background context to topics discussed in class, or in other cases will provide more detail to lecture topics or even extend the lecture discussion in other directions. Furthermore, textbook readings allow you to learn about other aspects of human geography that are not necessarily covered in lecture. In fact, much of what you will be asked to read in this course will not be discussed in lecture; this does not mean it is of lesser importance, but rather of equal (or greater) importance.

In some cases your Instructor will give you explicit guidance on how to approach specific sections of the readings. For example, in some cases your Instructor will ask you to 'skim' a chapter or a series of pages. What does this mean? Skimming usually means that the Instructor wants you to read the appropriate sections, but to not worry too much about the specific details enclosed within. Instead, you want to try to retain the most important concepts or points covered in that section of the reading. In practice, this process of skimming means that you read the section of the text and make only a handful of notes about the most important points.

In contrast to skimming, 'reading' usually means reading the textbook carefully and critically with the aim of retaining the information contained within. This usually entails making detailed notes, highlighting specific passages, and self-assessing your retention of the material. The textbook being used in this course has a free student resources section on its companion website which includes practice quizzes, study questions, and various mapping and related exercises designed to help assess how well you have retained what you have read and learned.

1.3.6   Avenue to Learn: Skeletal Outlines of Lectures

This course has an Avenue to Learn ('A2L' or 'Avenue') site, and materials will be deposited there regularly, and so you are encouraged to make use of this technology on a daily basis. An area of discussion has been set up where you can interact with fellow students about course materials. As part of this course, skeletal outlines of lectures will be available for downloading from Avenue to Learn on the day of class. It is important to stress, however, that while having these lecture notes ahead of time can be useful for structuring your own lecture notes and for reviewing course material before exams, there is NO substitute for attending class and to writing your own, more detailed notes - having these skeletal notes alone will be insufficient to pass this course. Making notes from what you see and hear in class is a critically important skill that you will need in order to succeed in university, but also for the rest of your life.

Some students may post their notes to Avenue to Learn for others that have missed class. A word of caution about relying on these notes is necessary: in some cases the notes may be incomplete or inaccurate. In addition, each student takes notes about what they think is important, not necessarily what is important. Therefore, relying on these notes, rather than taking your own is a huge risk. The best method for taking lecture notes is to attend lecture yourself!

Please note, while Avenue to Learn has an internal email function which allows you to email class-mates, do not use this function to email the entire class to request lecture notes for classes you have missed. **Students that send such emails may be suspended from Avenue to Learn (see section 1.10.6 of this manual).** *Instead, use the Avenue to Learn discussion forum, and in particular, the Lecture Exchange Forum.*

1.3.7   Summary:

What you get from a course depends on what you put into it. The responsibility is on you, the student, to do the required work before, during and after the lectures. This means reading the assigned textbook passages, taking good and appropriate notes during each and every lecture, and critically reflecting upon the content you hear in lecture and read in the textbook. Being a responsible student also means seeking assistance from your TA or Instructor when difficulties arise. Above all, remember that you should be concerned with more than just learning facts, i.e., you should also strive to develop critical thinking skills. This, you will probably find, will make your learning experiences more rewarding not just in geography, but in all your courses.

1.4 *Guide to Assignments*

In addition to attending lectures, being attentive and taking good notes during lectures, and supplementing lecture content by reading the assigned content from the course textbook, a significant proportion of student learning occurs through the completion of course assignments. This course has a number of assignments which are designed to help you develop critical transferrable skills such as critical thinking, research, analysis, interpretation, and field work. Some of these assignments will be completed individually, and others will involve some group work. This section provides some guidance on how you can maximize your learning via the course assignments.

The relative weighting of the assignments in this course is as follows:

Assignment	Percent of Final Mark
1	7
2	20

The basic assignment guidelines are included in Chapter 2 of this manual, but it should be noted that a major component of the tutorials in this course are dedicated to introducing you to these assignments, and in assisting you in developing the necessary skills to complete them. As such, attending the tutorials is of critical importance.

1.4.1 *Assignment Completion and Submission:*

Do not wait for the last minute to start your assignments! Not only can computers fail, but you will have no opportunity to reflect on your work. Hand everything in on time. When appropriate, staple your assignment and put your name and student number on it, using the sample cover page outlined in this chapter (section 1.4.5). Assignments are to be submitted directly to your TA in your tutorial or via the digital drop-box on Avenue to Learn.

If, for some reason, this is not possible, the assignment can be dropped in the *course-specific drop-box near the Geography office (GSB-206)* subject to penalty (see below). This box is emptied and material date stamped daily at 4:00 pm. It is critically important that your name, your TA's name and the course code is located on the cover page of the assignment. **Under no circumstances should the assignment be slid under an office door**. Make sure to always keep an extra copy of your assignment. The TA and Instructor are not responsible for lost assignments.

BE WARNED: If you choose to submit your Assignment via the physical drop-box a penalty of 5% will be imposed (assuming it is submitted in the drop-box on the day it is due and before 4:00 pm). Submissions can be made after 4:00 pm by using the 'night depository' at the western end of the second-floor of GSB. Assignments submitted via this drop-box will be received and date-stamped the next business day and additional late penalties (see section 1.4.2) will be imposed.

1.4.2   Late Assignments:

Assignments are due at the time stated and are to be submitted directly to your TA in your tutorial or via the Avenue to Learn drop-box. If you have a valid reason for tardiness, please discuss it with your Instructor before the due date. Having midterms and assignments due in other courses do not constitute valid excuses. **Keep in mind that accepting late assignments is based on the discretion of your Instructor – not your TA.** We reserve the right not to accept late assignments and assign you a mark of zero. All late assignments will be deducted 15% per day (weekends count as two days).

Note: Homework tasks (see section 1.5.3) are not to be submitted to the course drop-box (they will **not** be marked). These tasks are due in your tutorial and must be submitted directly to your TA.

1.4.3   Group Work:

Some assignments require you to work in groups. Group work is a critically important skill to develop over the course of your educational career, but it takes work (see chapter 4 of this courseware). In any employment environment you will be required to work in groups, and in most cases you will have little to no say in who your group-mates are, and little recourse for dealing with difficult group-mates. Group work assignments are designed to help you develop skills in managing your time, managing the time of the group, organization of tasks and responsibilities, and in social responsibility. Conflicts emerge in all groups; group members have different priorities and time commitments and dedication to the group effort. The best groups, however, are those that can deal with these conflicts internally and come up with resolutions. If your group has serious issues that cannot be resolved within the group itself, then you should speak to your TA. However, coming to your TA after an assignment is submitted to complain about the efforts of particular group-mates will be of little value, so raise your concerns before it is too late. Groups that are unable to work together successfully are subject to penalty.

1.4.4   General Guidelines for Assignments:

1. It is important that each assignment submitted under a student's name be her/his own. Consult the McMaster University Senate's "Academic Integrity Policy".

2. All assignments (unless specified otherwise) must be accompanied by an appropriate title page; see section 1.4.5 of this courseware for an example. This is the preferred form of title page for this course.

3. Students must type their work. Hand-written work will only be accepted in certain cases; you will be informed by your TA when it is acceptable to submit hand-written work.

4. The only acceptable type fonts are Times New Roman (12 point) and Arial (11 point). Margins must be 1 inch. **All work should be double-spaced.** Changing of margins/font sizes/line spacing to fit length requirements will not be tolerated.

5. Do not exceed the suggested maximum length for an answer. Be sure to include page numbers on all pages (except the title page).

6. Graphs and diagrams should have appropriate titles and labels.

7. Matters of style (referencing, etc.) are specified in the Referencing section of Chapter 3 (section 3.5) of this courseware. This style <u>must</u> be used in all assignments. There will be deductions on your assignment grade for not following this style.

8. Always reference the work of others in the text of your write-up and include a list of references, where appropriate. Not referencing the work of others is a form of academic dishonesty and will be handled appropriately. See Chapter 3 of this handbook for referencing specifics.

9. Always proof-read your work, checking for spelling and grammatical errors. A portion of your assignment grade is for writing quality and style.

10. Assignments must be submitted in tutorial (directly to the TA) or via the course Avenue to Learn drop-box. **E-mailed assignments will not be accepted**.

1.4.5 *Sample Title Page for Assignments:*

STUDENT # 123456789
STUDENT NAME: JOHN SMITH

GEOG 1HA3
Human Geographies: Society and Culture

Assignment 1
A meaningful title

Instructor's Name:
TA's Name:
Tutorial Day/Time:
Date of Submission:

1.4.6   Assignments - Considerations in Map Design:

Maps are a succinct form of communication since the user sees the entire message at once. Thus, the person designing the map has a responsibility to ensure that the map's intended message is actually portrayed. This is accomplished by focusing on eight key elements, emphasized in order of their hierarchical importance.

1.4.6.1   Eight Important Aspects of Map Design

1. **Message/body:** The message/body of a map is its content; the picture the creator aims to portray by producing it. When designing a map, the message should be the aspect that the user sees first, and should take up the majority of the space within the confines of the map.

2. **Title:** After the user has seen the content of a map, they may be interested in knowing more. The first means of giving the user some extra information is with a concise and comprehensive title,

3. **Legend:** The legend explains the components of the map. It should include any symbols, colours and abbreviations used in the map's message. Since the legend portrays quite detailed information, and is not needed for the user's initial observation, its hierarchical position is below the message and title. It should have an appropriate title (avoid "Legend").

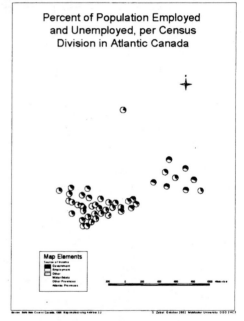

4. **North Arrow:** Often taken for granted, this map aspect is extremely important. A map can be rendered useless if it fails to provide the user with an idea of orientation.

5. **Scale:** A proper map should always have a fractional/numerical scale. Even sketch maps should be accompanied by an approximate scale.

6. **Border:** A border is important because it focuses the reader's attention towards the most important aspect of the map: the message. Other aspects like scale, north arrow and legend should be included within the border as well.

7. **Data Source:** The most common location for a reference to the source of the data used in the map is the lower left hand corner, just below the border. Here, the cartographer should list the source(s) of the data used in creating the map.

8. **Author:** Lastly, it is very important to include the author's (cartographer's) name, and the date the map was created. If a user wants to have more detailed information, they can contact the author/cartographer. The most common place for these names is the lower right hand corner of the map, just below the border.

1.5   *Guide to Tutorials & Homework Tasks*

In addition to lectures, textbook readings, and assignments, student learning in this course relies heavily on our small-group learning environments, known as tutorials. Students will meet most weeks for approximately two hours with a TA and a small group of other students. In tutorials students will be introduced to assignments, engage in topically relevant discussions, participate in engaging exercises, develop key course and transferable skills, etc. Attendance in tutorials is not only expected, it is of great benefit to the student through participation grades. In addition, students that attend tutorials generally do substantially better on their tests/exams and assignments. Not only this, but students that regularly attend tutorials report that they enjoy the course more than those that do not, and they indicate that they learn more as well.

1.5.1   *Tutorial Schedule*

Wk.:	Tut.:	Date:	Tutorial Topic & Discussion:	Assignment Issues:	Due Dates:
1		Jan. 5-8	*No Tutorials*		
2		Jan. 11-15	*No Tutorials*		
3	1	Jan. 18-22	**Introduction to Tutorials**		
4	2	Jan. 25-29	**Geographic Skills & Map Library**	Assignment 1 (introduced)	Assignment 1 Due
5	3	Feb. 1-5	**Research Skills & Cultural Regions**		
6	4	Feb. 8-12	**Population Issues**		
7		Feb 15-19	*No Tutorials – Reading Break*		
8	5	Feb. 22-26	**Health Geography**	Assignment 2 (introduced)	
9	6	Feb. 29-Mar. 4	**Fieldwork Skills**		
10	7	Mar. 7-11	**Urban Landscapes**		
11	8	Mar. 14-18	**Cultural Landscapes**		
12	9	Mar. 21-25	**Cultural & Political Issues**		
13	10	Mar. 28-Apr. 1	**Exam Review & Tutorial Wrap-Up**		Assignment 2 Due
14		Apr. 4-8	*No Tutorials – End of Classes*		

1.5.2   *Tutorial Attendance and Participation:*

Tutorials are an integral part of this course. Attendance is crucial to your successful completion of the assignments and to your success in the course. Your TA will take attendance at each tutorial. Tutorial Attendance will be rewarded with a bonus mark added to your final grade. As this is a "bonus" mark, even excused absences (i.e. illness) will count towards tutorials missed. The following is how the Tutorial Attendance bonus will be rewarded:

Student Tutorial Attendance:	Bonus Marks:
Absent from 0 or 1 Tutorial in the semester	3 Bonus Marks (i.e. one grade point)
Absent from 2 Tutorials in the semester	2 Bonus Marks
Absent from 3 Tutorials in the semester	1 Bonus Mark
Absent from more than 3 Tutorials in the semester	0 Bonus Marks

In addition to attendance, participation will also be graded. This **participation mark (18%)** will be **part** of your final grade. 'Participation' is different than 'showing up'; participation means actively engaging in in-class activities, coming to tutorials prepared, and showing enthusiasm for group and individual activities. In addition to receiving crucial assignment information, in your tutorial your TA will be guiding you through a series of tutorial exercises. These exercises are meant to assist you with your assignments, enhance course content, and provide some instruction on aspects of being a university student. Some of these exercises will be completed during class-time, while others will require some work at home. The section below (1.5.3) outlines some of these in-class and home-based tutorial exercises (Homework Tasks).

If you miss a tutorial for medical reasons, you should go to the Office of the Associate Dean (of your Faculty) – do NOT use an MSAF for missed tutorials (see section 1.7.3). The Associate Dean's office will then notify your Instructor about your absence. At this time you *may* be able to get any tutorial exercises/homework tasks you missed from your TA.

1.5.3   Homework Tasks:

Coming to tutorial prepared to be an active participant is crucial to your learning experience. As part of this preparation, we have developed a number of very simple, and not at all time-consuming, 'homework tasks' which are designed to help you get the most out of your tutorial experience. Some of these tasks are to be completed at home prior to your tutorial, others will be completed during your tutorial, and others still will ask you to reflect upon things that you have just completed in your tutorial. These tasks are graded, and your grades contribute towards your tutorial participation mark. The table below outlines the homework tasks we have developed for this course, and provides a little information about what you are expected to do.

HW Task #	Homework Task Title:	In-Class Activity or Homework:	Submitted:
1	Student Responsibility Contract	Homework (Online Quiz)	Avenue (Quiz)
2	Academic Integrity	Homework (Online Quiz)	Avenue (Quiz)
3	Research Skills	Homework	Avenue (Drop-Box)
4	Critical Evaluation of Sources	In-Class Activity	In-Class (TA)
5	Cultural Regions	In-Class Activity	In-Class (TA)
6	Spatial Analytical Tools	Homework (Reflection)	Avenue (Drop-Box)
7	Health-Care Debate Research	Homework	In-Class (TA)
8	Population Issues	Homework (Reflection)	Avenue (Drop-Box)
9	Health-Care Debate	Homework (Reflection)	Avenue (Drop-Box)
10	Hamilton Image	Homework (Reflection)	Avenue (Drop-Box)
11	Fieldwork	In-Class Activity	In-Class (TA)
12	GIS Maps & Interpretation	Homework	Avenue (Drop-Box)
13	Political 'Hot Topics'	In-Class Activity	In-Class (TA)

1.5.4 Grading of Homework Tasks:

As mentioned above, these homework tasks will be graded. However, the grading system we use for these tasks is different from most traditional marking schemes. The grading scale used here is called the E-A-S-I-O system, and grades are assessed as follows:

Grade	Expectations/Reason for Grade
E (Excellent)	exceptional effort / work far exceeds expectations
A (Average)	well done / followed guidelines and met expectations
S (Satisfactory)	work completed with some effort/thought, but does not meet expectations
I (Insufficient)	minimal effort / not completed
O ('0' / Zero)	not submitted / no grade

Some homework tasks are completion-based, meaning that if you complete them, then you get credit for having done so. Although not evaluated in the same way as other homework tasks, the completion of these tasks is **expected** and will comprise part of your tutorial participation grade. These completion-based homework tasks will be evaluated as follows:

Evaluation	Expectations/Reason for Grade
C (Complete)	completed in full / well done
I (Incomplete)	not completed in full / minimal effort
NS (Not Submitted)	not submitted / no completion credit

Individually, each homework task is worth between 0-2% of your course grade. Homework tasks must be submitted in tutorial directly to your TA or, in some cases, to the Avenue to Learn drop-box; homework tasks submitted to the physical course drop box in GSB will not be marked. Finally, grades for homework tasks may not be appealed (see section 1.9.3); you may discuss your grade with your TA, but you may not request it to be re-marked.

1.5.5 Grades Assigned by TAs:

At the end of term each student is required to check with her/his TA, or the IA to ensure that all marks have been properly recorded on Avenue to Learn. There is a period of time prior to the exam which is available to resolve any issues with your grades. This is not a period to ask for your assignment to be remarked or discussing any student absence issues, but rather for correcting any errors that may appear on the official grade record.

1.6   Guide to Tests & Exams

Tests and exams in this course will examine material from the lectures, tutorials, discussions, individual and group assignments and the textbook, so you need to be prepared. Below are a few tips on getting prepared for your tests & exams, as well as some suggestions for how to actually write them.

1.6.1   Preparation & Studying:

Everyone has a different studying style. One of the most difficult parts of being in first year is discovering what <u>you</u> need to do in order to study efficiently and effectively. Some people need music, some people need quiet. Some can just read and memorize, some must take endless study notes. Try different approaches to see what fits <u>you</u> best.

Without question organization is key! First, make sure you have all the lecture notes and have completed all the required readings. It would be a wise strategy to write out all the definitions and key concepts. Write these on a separate sheet or on cue-cards and focus your last minute studying on the concepts that you are having the most difficulty with. Use highlighters, different coloured pens or post-it notes to organize your study notes.

Simply reading the material passively is not an effective way to study for this course. Most of the concepts in this course are not difficult to understand, however there are many of them. So, simply reading them will only go so far. You need to learn (and retain) the material. In order to do this you need to write out the definitions/concepts and develop practice questions for yourself. Try writing out definitions, identifying items on a map, and sketching diagrams. Practice, Practice, Practice!

Learning the course content takes time and preparation. Despite what others tell you (or what might have worked in high school) cramming does not work! Material is best learned through repetition, and that is why students who attend lecture always do better on the exams than those who do not. This is because, i) they hear the material from the Instructor, ii) they see it on the screen, iii) they write down notes (hopefully), and iv) they then study the material at home. True learning of the material does take time!

When preparing for the test or exam, be sure to learn what the format will be. For example, how many questions will be of the 'multiple choice' or 'true & false' variety, how many will require written answers, and how long are your answers expected to be. This should give you some clues as to the level of detail expected by the Instructor, which can help you to determine the most appropriate way to study.

1.6.2   Writing the Test or Exam:

When writing the test, time management is important. When you first sit down, take a moment or two to review the whole test or exam to see what you will be required to do. Then, portion your time accordingly; don't leave a heavily-weighted question (that you know the answer to) until the very end and then risk running out of time. Try and answer the easiest questions first –

this can be a big boost to your confidence.

During the test, read the questions carefully and take time to think about what is being asked. In so doing, consider what is the most efficient and appropriate way to answer. One of the best ways of demonstrating to the person marking your test or exam that you truly understand the concepts is to provide appropriate examples whenever possible. When you complete the test take time to review all your answers and repeatedly ask yourself "DID I ANSWER THE QUESTION?"

Finally, many courses today include multiple choice questions as part of their tests and exams. While there are many resources available to help you learn how to best answer multiple choice questions (visit the Centre for Student Development for some handy reference materials) one very simple technique to insure success is to make sure your multiple choice questions get marked. Unfortunately, many students fail to properly fill in their multiple choice (Scantron) sheets, and therefore risk not having their tests or exams marked. Below is an example of a properly completed Scantron sheet. Be sure that you always record the following information on your Scantron sheets:

- **Your FIRST name and your LAST name**
- **Your student number**
- **The course code and name, and the name of the Instructor (if appropriate)**
- **Your student number using the seven columns of circular bubbles under the heading 'Student Number'**
- **The test/exam version using the column of circular bubbles under the heading 'Version'**

1.6.3   Example - OMR/Scantron Sheet for Multiple Choice Questions on Tests & Exams:

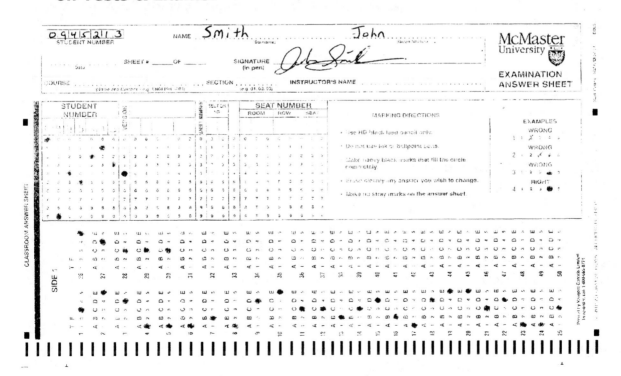

1.7   Policies on Student Absences

Student absences from lecture, tutorial, test, etc. can be the result of any number of particular circumstances, some of which are major and some which are more minor. In this course, the protocol for what to do in the case of being absent varies depending on the component of the course that you have missed. The sub-sections below outline what to do if your absence affects your ability to complete an assignment (section 1.7.1), write a test (section 1.7.2), attend a lecture or tutorial (section 1.7.3), or submit a tutorial-based homework task (section 1.7.3).

1.7.1   Student Absence: Assignments

In case of a student absence (i.e. illness or other extraordinary circumstance) that affects the completion or submission of an *assignment*, please ensure that you complete the following steps. Never assume that, even after following these steps, marks will automatically be re-allocated to other areas of evaluation; the work must still be completed. And, please note that *accommodations for missed work will never be made unless you meet with your Instructor* – simply submitting documentation is insufficient.

Please note: due to the length of time given to complete Assignment #2, combined with the fact that it is a group assignment, MSAFs may not be used for this assignment.

1.7.1.1   Student Absence of Three (3) Days or Less

Students seeking accommodations for an absence of three days or less (e.g. a minor or moderate illness) normally do not need to provide documentary evidence. Students should use the McMaster Student Absence Form (MSAF) which is an on-line, self-reporting tool. You can access the MSAF via MOSAIC. Your Instructor will automatically be notified of your request for accommodations.

IMPORTANT: Once you have completed the on-line form, it is then your responsibility to meet with (*in person*) your Instructor. Your Instructor has office hours set aside for conducting these sorts of meetings. Please note, it is entirely at the discretion of the Instructor to accommodate (or not) your absence. Failure to meet with your Instructor within **two weeks** of the submitted MSAF will result in an automatic grade of zero on that portion(s) of the course assessment.

1.7.1.2   Student Absence of Greater Than Three (3) Days

Students seeking accommodations for an absence lasting longer than three days **may not** use the on-line self-reporting tool. In such cases, you MUST report to the office of the Associate Dean of your Faculty (e.g. Social Science, Business, Engineering, etc.). Normally, you will be required to provide supporting documentation, i.e. a McMaster University Medical Form or appropriate documentation of verifiable origin. Be sure that your documentation clearly specifies the length of the illness or absence. Your Instructor will be notified by your Faculty Office (normally within 24 hours) if/when your absence has been approved.

IMPORTANT: Once you have completed this process in the Associate Dean's office, it is then your responsibility to meet with (***in person***) your Instructor to discuss the nature of your absence and the accommodations sought. Your Instructor has office hours set aside for conducting these sorts of meetings. Please note, it is entirely at the discretion of the Instructor to accommodate (or not) your absence. Failure to meet with your Instructor within **two weeks** of submitting your request for relief will result in an automatic grade of zero on that portion(s) of the course assessment.

1.7.1.3   Additional Notes Regarding Student Absence

Students may submit only one MSAF ***per term*** (**not per course**) for relief/accommodations for missed course work due to absence. Any student seeking relief for missed work more than once in a term will be required to meet with an academic advisor in the office of the Associate Dean of your Faculty (e.g. Social Science, Business, Engineering, etc.).

IMPORTANT: All students seeking accommodation for missed work due to an absence (regardless of length) must meet with their Instructor promptly. When you meet with your Instructor you will be discussing what accommodations will be made for your absence (i.e. extension of deadline, etc.). Do not assume that marks will automatically be re-allocated to other parts of the course. **Please note, emails/phone calls are not sufficient; you must see the Instructor IN PERSON. You may not go to your TA or the IA for these matters.**

1.7.2   Student Absence: Mid-Term Test

In this course, the Mid-Term test is being held outside of normal class time (i.e. on **Saturday February 6th, 2016**). Because of this, special policies are in place for students that cannot write their test at the designated time. Please read the following policies carefully.

1.7.2.1   Students that cannot write the Mid-Term during the designated time due to an academic, work, family, or extracurricular conflict

If, for some reason (i.e. academic, work, family, athletic or other extracurricular commitments) a student cannot write the Mid-Term test during the designated time, they may formally request to write the test at the '***early write***' time, which for this course is **Thursday February 4th, 2016 (8:30-10:00 PM)**. Students wishing to write at the earlier time must submit an 'early write' petition before **4:00 PM on Monday February 1st, 2016**. Failure to submit a petition by this date means that the student has forfeited their right to request an early write of the test.

1.7.2.2   Students that are unable to write the test at either the designated time, or the 'early write' time

If, for some reason (i.e. illness, conflict, etc.) a student cannot write the Mid-Term test during either the designated time or the 'early write' time, they must submit an MSAF (or get Faculty-approval) as per the Student Absence policies as stated in **section 1.7.1** (1.7.1.1 or 1.7.1.2) with one exception; ***the student will not be permitted to write a make-up test***. In the case of a missed Mid-Term test, the weighting of the test will be shifted to the Final Exam.

IMPORTANT: Students seeking a re-weighting of their grades due to a missed Mid-Term must meet with their Instructor promptly (within two weeks of the date of the Mid-Term). When you meet with your Instructor you will be discussing what accommodations will be made for your absence. Do not assume that marks will automatically be re-allocated to other parts of the course; you must meet with your Instructor to discuss this. **Please note, emails/phone calls are not sufficient; you must see the Instructor IN PERSON. You may <u>not</u> go to your TA or IA for these matters.**

1.7.3   Student Absence: Lectures, Tutorials and Homework Tasks

In this course you may **<u>not</u>** submit an MSAF for a missed lecture, tutorial or homework task; MSAFs will only be accepted for assignments or the Mid-Term test. Students that miss a lecture are responsible for finding out what they missed from a fellow student in the class, and are responsible for getting their own set of lecture notes (try the Avenue to Learn discussion forum for this).

Students that miss a tutorial and/or are unable to submit a homework task because of their student absence forfeit their tutorial attendance mark for that day, and/or may lose out on marks for tutorial participation.

1.8   Grades and Grade Expectations

Many first-year students, as well as upper-year students from outside the Faculty of Social Science, have pre-conceived notions of the grades they expect to get in courses. It is our experience that these pre-conceived ideas are often far different from reality. It is not that 'As' are unachievable, to the contrary. Many students will do very well in their courses, this one included, and many others will excel and achieve grades of 'A' or even 'A+'. Having said that, these grades are not easy to achieve; students must work hard, come to class regularly, and demonstrate true higher-level thinking and effort to achieve those grades. Students that go through the motions, attend class irregularly, do not put in an honest effort in class or tutorial will generally earn grades that reflect this approach and attitude.

1.8.1   Grade Expectations:

Below is a rough outline of <u>our</u> expectations for student achievement in this course. Your TA will give you more explicit expectations for each assignment.

Letter Grade (range)	Qualities, characteristics	Approx. % of students
A (A- to A+)	A truly hard-earned grade. A VERY good student, one that demonstrates exceptional effort, diligent research skills, thoughtful and higher-level thinking and analysis. Student will have attended >90% of classes and tutorials and will have participated actively.	About 10-15%
B (B- to B+)	A good, solid student performance. Students in this category demonstrate slightly above average work. The student's work is solid, but not exceptional. The student has exhibited obvious effort, but perhaps struggled on one or two aspects of the course (e.g. a poor Mid-Term or Final Exam, or poor effort on a group assignment, etc.). This is a grade to be proud of.	About 25-35%
C (C- to C+)	A slightly below average performance. While the student has demonstrated some effort, they have missed a few too many classes or tutorials, and more than a couple of the marked components of the course were below expectations. The most obvious shortcoming of students in this category are those that don't put in the extra effort to improve their writing skills or their test-writing and studying skills. Students that leave their work to the last minute often fall into this category.	About 20%
D (D- to D+)	The student's performance is poor, and far below expectations. Clearly, the effort was sub-par, and the student did not attend enough classes or tutorials in order to follow instructions on assignments correctly. Student time-management is often a problem here as well; the student gets overwhelmed at certain times of the year and then either does not submit assignments, or submits them very late, or submits them of such poor quality that the grade is very low.	About 10%-20%
F	An unacceptable effort. The work submitted is below university standards. The student needs to remedy their work habits in order to continue.	Hard to say. Hopefully no more than 5% to 10% at the most.

1.9   Policies on Mark Appeals

If you have concerns about a mark given on an assignment, your Mid-Term, or on a homework task, please review your work, and especially the feedback provided by your TA, before you request it to be remarked. The protocols for appealing a grade on submitted work varies depending on the type of work; please review the appropriate section(s) below.

1.9.1   Assignment Mark Appeals:

Assignments in this course take one of two forms; traditional assignments that students submit to their TA after several weeks of work, and tutorial-based assignments which students submit at the end of a single tutorial period.

For the traditional assignments, you may request your work be remarked by providing a brief written summary of why you think your assignment should be remarked. The person who originally marked the assignment (i.e. your TA) will remark your assignment. Do not request that the Instructor remark an assignment without first speaking to your TA; the Instructor will simply return the assignment to your TA. To submit your assignment for remarking, complete the Mark Appeal form and attach it to your assignment and submit it to your TA during the assignment viewing periods. Please allow two weeks for processing and remarking.

For the tutorial-based assignments you will be provided with an opportunity in which you can come in and review your assignment and consider the grade assigned. If, during this review period, you believe that you were not properly awarded marks on particular sections of the assignment, you may submit a Mark Appeal form. All assignment mark appeals will be processed by your TA. Your entire assignment will be reassessed and, as such, your mark may either go up or down.

1.9.2   Mid-Term Test Mark Appeals:

In this course, you will not get your tests back, but will be provided with an opportunity in which you can come in and review your test and consider the grade assigned. If, during this review period, you believe that you were not properly awarded marks on a particular question, you may submit a Mark Appeal form. All Mid-Term mark appeals will be processed by the Instructional Assistant (not your TA). As always, your entire test will be reassessed and, as such, your mark may either go up or down.

1.9.3   Homework Task Mark Appeals:

Homework tasks may not be re-submitted for mark appeal. However, you are encouraged to speak with your TA to discuss the rationale for the marks assigned on these tasks.

1.10   Being a Student in Human Geography

You are at McMaster University to learn; your professor, your TA, and the course IA are here to assist you in your learning process. However, it is important that you keep in mind that they are ordinary people, just like you; thus, mutual respect is expected.

Furthermore, your fellow students are also here to learn, and have the right to do so without disruption or interference from other students. In order to foster an environment of collegiality amongst all students and instructional staff (Instructor, TAs, IA), please keep the following guidelines in mind.

Please note that these guidelines are in addition to McMaster University's Student Code of Conduct policy. This code of conduct policy can be accessed via the following web address:

- http://www.mcmaster.ca/policy/Students-AcademicStudies/StudentCode.pdf

1.10.1 In the Classroom:

To be successful in this course, you need to come to class (lecture and tutorials) regularly, or you will miss in-class activities and explanations of assignments, homework, etc. When we do activities in class, participate. Get to know people. Use the opportunity to think and learn about the material. Remember, your learning is your responsibility - keep up with readings, attend lectures and take detailed notes.

1.10.2 Behaviour:

In-class questions are not disruptions, but opportunities to expand upon issues raised in lecture or the textbook. Please do not be shy with questions or comments. You are encouraged to be engaged, but you must also be respectful. You should avoid disrespectful disruptions such as coming to class late, leaving early, using a cell phone, using a laptop for activities not related to the course, talking to your neighbours, etc. This behaviour interferes with other students' opportunities to learn. Remember: you are not invisible - the Instructor and other students can see you talking, can see your laptop screen, see what you are reading, and are bothered by your disruptive behaviours. This kind of behaviour is unacceptable, and students who partake in it may be asked to leave the classroom/tutorial room.

1.10.3 Use of Laptop Computers, Smartphones, Tablets, etc.:

Electronic devices such as laptop computers, smartphones, tablets, etc. are now ubiquitous on university campuses. These devices can be of great benefit to students in class for taking notes, etc. But at the same time they can be a tremendous distraction, not only to the individual using the device, but also to those sitting nearby. It is tempting to momentarily switch from taking notes to read an email, or send a text message, or check social media. This temptation should be resisted; not only does this activity break your concentration from what is happening in class, but it is tremendously difficult for those sitting around you to not get distracted as well.

A recent Hamilton Spectator article (2013) outlined the findings of an American study about the perils of student distraction in class via electronic devices; it is worth a read:

- http://www.thespec.com/news-story/2873732-put-away-that-cellphone-student/

No electronic devices are needed for any of the activities that take place in tutorials. As such, we reserve the right to request that you not bring your electronic devices to tutorial and/or we may prohibit their use in tutorial.

Students that have a disability that requires their use of such devices may get an exemption (in certain circumstances) from the Instructor. In order to protect student privacy, if you need to seek an exemption to this 'no electronic devices in tutorial' policy, please do not have this conversation with your TA.

1.10.4 Assistance:

Please, do not be afraid to ask for help. Your TA, the course IA and your Instructor will gladly assist you with any problems you may be experiencing. If you are finding yourself lost in the coursework, ask right away; neither your TA, IA nor your Instructor will be prepared to give you an overview of the course two weeks before the end of term! Bonus points and extra work for students that fall behind will NOT be available; thus, you must be prepared to ask questions as soon as you need the help.

1.10.5 E-mail Etiquette and Communication:

McMaster University policy now requires that **all** e-mail communication between a student and their Instructor, TA or IA, must be via their McMaster e-mail account. This policy is designed to protect student privacy.

Contacting your TA and/or Instructor electronically is fine for basic questions (i.e. confirming the time of a tutorial or scheduling an appointment). E-mail is not appropriate for asking detailed questions (i.e. missing a tutorial and wanting detailed instructions as to how to do your assignment). Such questions should be reserved for a scheduled appointment or office hours. Furthermore, TAs and Instructors will not respond to e-mail over weekends or late in the evening. Do not send e-mails the night before an assignment is due and expect a prompt response.

Please be courteous in your use of e-mail. Please ensure that your full name and student number are included in your e-mail. There are basic social conventions that govern all forms of communication, and this includes e-mail. Try to assume that your Instructor or TA is a potential employer and construct your e-mails accordingly. Use of "texting" techniques/shorthand, etc. will NOT be tolerated; your Instructor and TA reserve the right to ignore (not respond to) e-mails which are improperly composed. Finally, to insure prompt attention to your e-mail, and to avoid problems with spam filters, **please place "GEOG 1HA3" in the subject heading of all course-related e-mail.**

Please note, while Avenue to Learn has an internal e-mail function which allows you to e-mail class-mates, etc., in this course the following two rules apply: 1) do not send e-mails to your Instructor, IA or TA via the this e-mail function – please use your regular McMaster University e-mail account, and 2) do not send e-mails to the entire class via this e-mail function – failure to abide by this rule is subject to possible suspension from Avenue to Learn.

1.10.6 *Avenue to Learn:*

Avenue to Learn is a tremendous resource for this course, and many others. Quick access to class news, skeletal lecture notes, grades, discussion areas, etc., are just a few of the many benefits. However, this system has its challenges as well, and as a result we have developed a couple of simple policies that govern your use of system for this course.

First, as mentioned in a couple of other places in this manual already, Avenue to Learn has an e-mail function. You may use this to e-mail a classmate, friend or partner for a group assignment if you wish, but you may not e-mail your Instructor, your TA or the course IA via the Avenue to Learn e-mail facility; your message will not be answered.

Second, you must not use the Avenue to Learn e-mail facility to send a message to the entire class; in the past, students have tried this in order to get copies of lecture notes that they are missing. This behaviour is incredibly annoying to the hundreds of students in the class, and as such, it will not be tolerated. Students that violate this rule may have their Avenue to Learn privileges suspended.

Third, the discussion forums on Avenue to Learn are monitored. Students that post inappropriate messages to these forums may have their Avenue to Learn privileges suspended. If you are the victim of an inappropriate post, or if you see one that you feel is inappropriate, please bring this to the attention of the course Instructional Assistant immediately.

Finally, it is the responsibility of all students to check the Avenue to Learn site for this course regularly. New material will be posted there on a daily basis, and it is your responsibility to be aware of the content that is posted there.

1.11 *Academic Integrity*

Cases of academic dishonesty, unfortunately, have been on the increase at universities in Canada and the United States in recent years. McMaster University and the School of Geography & Earth Sciences consider this to be a very serious issue indeed. In this course you will be educated about what does and does not constitute academic dishonesty. It is our hope that you, as a student; will conduct yourself in this course (and in all other courses) with the utmost in integrity.

According to McMaster University, academic dishonesty consists of misrepresentation by deception or by other fraudulent means and can result in serious consequences, e.g. the grade of zero on an assignment, loss of credit with a notation on the transcript (notation reads: "Grade of F assigned for academic dishonesty"), and/or suspension or expulsion from the university.

It is your responsibility to understand what constitutes academic dishonesty. For information on the various kinds of academic dishonesty please refer to the Academic Integrity Policy, specifically Appendix 3, located at http://www.mcmaster.ca/senate/academic/ac_integrity.htm

The following illustrates only three forms of academic dishonesty:
- Plagiarism, e.g. the submission of work that is not one's own or for which other credit has been obtained.
- Improper collaboration in group work.
- Copying or using unauthorized aids in tests and examinations.

In this course, we will provide you with guidance and instruction on what is, and what is not, academic dishonesty. We will do this in a number of different ways, for example, via an online learning module, a quiz, some exercises and discussions in tutorial, and so on. While we will do our best to educate you about doing academic work with integrity, it is ultimately up to you to learn about this, and to conduct yourself with the utmost of integrity at all times.

2.0 Tutorial Materials & Assignments

2.1 Tutorial Information and Assignments

For each weekly tutorial there is a dedicated section in your courseware. Please read this information **prior** to attending your tutorial. Certain weeks feature a 'preparation' section in which you are to read/complete a task prior to attending your tutorial. The more prepared you are for your tutorial, the more you will get out of it. Also, remember that there is a participation mark in the course, and this mark is partially derived from your preparation for these tutorials.

There are blank sections in the weekly tutorial instructions in which it is expected that you take notes on the material your TA gives you. In addition, the actual assignment pages are relatively short, and your TA will give you much more guidance in tutorial.

2.2   *Tutorial 1: Week of January 18-22, 2016*

- Preparation:
  - o   Purchase and bring Courseware

- Assignments:
  - o   *None*

- Tutorial Activities:
  - o   Ice-Breaker Activity
  - o   Tutorial Introduction & Overview
  - o   Tips for Success
  - o   How Well Do You Know Your World (***Google Earth***)? Group Activity

- Courseware Readings:
  - o   Chapter 1 – Course Information & Policies
  - o   Student Responsibility Contract (section 2.2.1)

●———●

Ice-Breaker Activity:

My THREE people:

1.

2.

3.

●———●

Teaching Assistant (TA) and Instructional Assistant (IA) Contact Information:

TA Name: _____   **IA Name:** _____

TA Email: _____   **IA Email:** _____

TA Office Hours: _____   **IA Office Hours:** _____

●———●

Notes on Course and Tutorial Organization: *Things that I need to know and remember ...*

- **Assignments**

- **Tutorial Schedule/Tutorial Attendance**

    o **Tutorial Participation**

    o **Homework Tasks**

- **Student Absences (MSAF and Faculty Approved)**

- **Being a Student in Human Geography**

    o **Electronic Devices**

- **Student Responsibility Contract**

    o *Section 2.2.1 of this courseware outlines the Student Responsibility Contract (SRC) for this course*
    o *Part of your homework this week (Homework Task #1) is to log-in to Avenue to Learn and play our Course/Tutorial Organization and Course Policies Slideshow – look under 'Content' and 'Tutorial Materials'*
        - *You are strongly encouraged to follow along with Chapter One of your courseware. There is space in the Tutorial #1 section to make notes.*
    o *When you have viewed the slideshow, take the online quiz which corresponds to this Student Responsibility Contract (under 'Assessments' and 'Quizzes').*
        - *Completion of the quiz is equivalent to signing this contract. Assignment marks will NOT be released to you until you have completed the quiz.*
    o *Deadline to complete this quiz: January 25th (8:00 am)*

Tips for Success in this Course: *Skills I should develop ...*

In-Class (Group) Activity: *How Well Do You Know Your World (Google Earth)?*

Welcome to the School of Geography & Earth Sciences' 3-D Visualization Lab (the GEOCave)

What is Google Earth?

What can you do with Google Earth?

Activity:
- With your partner(s), try to identify each of the twelve human landscapes as they are revealed, clue by clue, by your TA.
- Note the name of each landscape in the table below, and make a few notes about what clues were key to your being able to identify the landscape (or not).
- Also, plot the location of each landscape on the world map (next page)

Landscape:	What Clues Gave it Away?
A -	
B -	
C -	
D -	
E -	
F -	
G -	
H -	
I -	
J -	
K -	
L -	

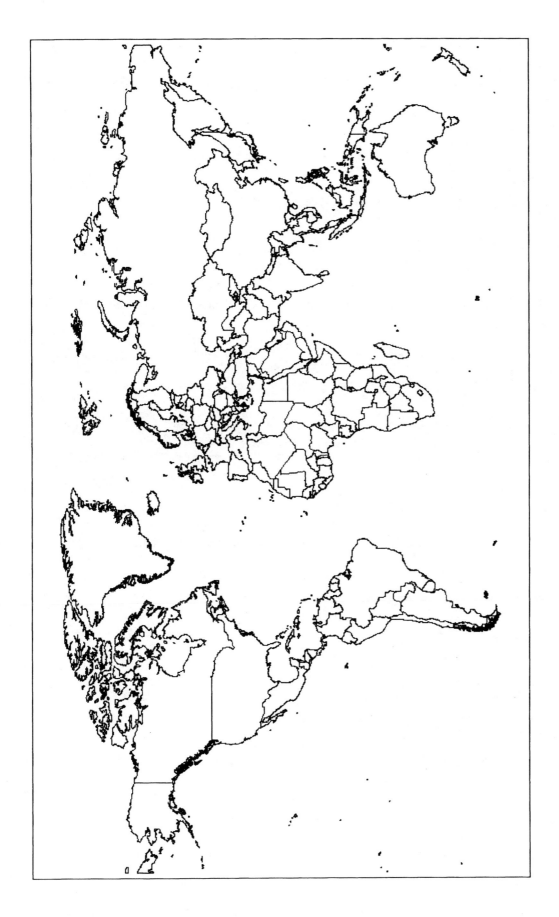

Reflection: *How well do you know your world?*

- Based on this activity, how well do you feel you know the world?

- Which places of the world were harder to identify and which places were easier? Why do you think this was?

Over the next three months your awareness of the world will improve, and your understanding of geography and the importance of place will become more complete ...

Notes from Slideshow on Course/Tutorial Organization and Course Policies: *Things that I need to know and remember ...*

- **Course Outline: Dates, etc.**

- **Lectures & Readings**

- **Assignments**

- **Tutorial Schedule/Tutorial Attendance**

  - **Tutorial Participation**

  - **Homework Tasks**

Notes from Slideshow on Course/Tutorial Organization and Course Policies (*Continued*):

- **Tests & Exams**

- **Student Absences (MSAF and Faculty Approved)**

  o **Assignments**

  o **Mid-Term**

  o **Lectures, Tutorials & Homework Tasks**

- **Grades & Grade Expectations**

- **Mark Appeals**

  o **Assignments**

  o **Mid-Term**

  o **Homework Tasks**

Notes from Slideshow on Course/Tutorial Organization and Course Policies (*Continued*)**:**

- **Being a Student in Human Geography**

  - **Electronic Devices**

  - **E-mail Etiquette**

  - **Avenue to Learn**

- **Student Responsibility Contract**

  - *Section 2.2.1 of this courseware outlines the Student Responsibility Contract (SRC) for this course*
  - *Part of your homework this week (Homework Task #1) is to log-in to Avenue to Learn and play our Course/Tutorial Organization and Course Policies Slideshow – look under 'Content' and 'Tutorial Materials'*
    - *You are strongly encouraged to follow along with Chapter One of your courseware. There is space in the Tutorial #1 section to make notes.*
  - *When you have viewed the slideshow, take the online quiz which corresponds to this Student Responsibility Contract (under 'Assessments' and 'Quizzes').*
    - *Completion of the quiz is equivalent to signing this contract. Assignment marks will NOT be released to you until you have completed the quiz.*
  - *Deadline to complete this quiz: January 25th (8:00 am)*

Academic Integrity

- o *Section 1.11 of this courseware outlines some of the basic principles of Academic Integrity. Further information can be found on the McMaster Academic Integrity website: www.mcmaster.ca/academicintegrity*
- o *In this course, we place tremendous emphasis on students doing honest work. In order to better understand what this means, part of your homework this week (Homework Task #2) is to log-in to Avenue to Learn and play our Academic Integrity Slideshow – look under 'Content' and 'Tutorial Materials'*
  - ▪ *There is space in the Tutorial #1 section to make notes.*
- o *When you have viewed the slideshow, take the online quiz (under 'Assessments' and 'Quizzes').*
  - ▪ *All students must successfully complete the Academic Integrity quiz in order to continue in this course. Assignment and test marks will NOT be released to you until you have completed the quiz. Your grade on this quiz will count towards your Tutorial Participation grade.*
- o *Deadline to complete this quiz: January 25th (8:00 am)*

Notes from Academic Integrity Slideshow: *Why is this so important, and what do I need to know …*

Notes on Academic Integrity Slideshow (*Continued*):

Notes on Academic Integrity Slideshow (*Continued*):

Notes: Homework Tasks and Preparation for Next Tutorial:

2.2.1 GEOG 1HA3 - Student Responsibility Contract:

Being a university student requires you to assume a level of responsibility towards your academic career. Rules and Regulations regarding coursework change during the transition from high school to university as well as varying between Faculties and courses at McMaster. We want to ensure that you (the student) understand and acknowledge certain aspects of how this course operates.

During the first tutorial, your TA will provide you with crucial information on the operation of this course. At the conclusion of this tutorial, you must review each section below to insure that you understand the information given and that you are aware of our course policies.

When finished, log-in to Avenue to Learn and complete the online quiz that corresponds to the Student Responsibility Contract (SRC). Completion of the quiz is equivalent to signing this contract. *You will not receive marks for assignments until you have satisfactorily completed this quiz (submitted this contract).*

2.2.1.1 Assignment Submission and Late Assignments:

Assignments are due at the beginning of my tutorial (unless stated otherwise). Assignments are to be submitted in person to my TA or to the Avenue to Learn drop-box (as specified by my TA).

There is a drop-box on the 2nd floor of GSB in which I can submit an assignment if I am unable to attend my tutorial. Any assignment submitted after 4:00 pm on the due date is considered late and will be deducted 15% per day; weekends result in a 30% deduction.

I need to communicate and make arrangements with my TA if I need (or wish) to hand in an assignment early. The Instructor, IA, and TA's are not responsible for the loss of assignments that are submitted in the drop-off box.

2.2.1.2 Tutorial Attendance, Participation & Homework Tasks:

Tutorials are held to enhance the lectures, as well as to provide essential information for my assignments. If I miss a tutorial, it is my responsibility to acquire the necessary information from classmates. It is not the TA's responsibility to go over the entire tutorial with me.

Tutorial participation, which includes some work to be completed at home between tutorials, is expected. In total 18%, of my course grade depends on my participation. Tutorial Attendance marks will be awarded as a Bonus for this course. Bonus marks up to 3% will be awarded on top of my course grade based on my attendance.

2.2.1.3 Mid-Term:

The mid-term will be written outside of class-time, on a Saturday, and in various locations across campus. It is my responsibility to know where I am to write my mid-term and to attend the test on time.

If I am unable to write the mid-term due to a previous commitment, I may apply to write the test early. In order to be eligible to write the test early, I must submit a petition to my Instructor, no less than 3 days prior to the early test date. No make-up mid-terms will be permitted.

2.2.1.4   Student Absence:

If I am ill, away from campus, or am unable to complete coursework (e.g. submit an assignment or write the mid-term) for any reason which has a duration of three days or less, than I should complete the on-line, self-declared form known as the McMaster Student Absence Form (MSAF).

If the duration of my absence is greater than three days, I must visit the office of the Associate Dean of my Faculty. I realize that I will likely be required to provide documentation for my absence in this case.

In either case (an absence up to, or in excess of, three days) it is my responsibility, to meet with my Instructor during their office hours to discuss what, if any, accommodations will be made for the missed work. I understand that phoning or emailing the Instructor is insufficient; I must see the Instructor during their office hours. I have two weeks from the date of submitting documentation to complete this process; otherwise I will receive a mark of zero.

Furthermore, I am not to assume that I do not have to complete any missed work; it is up to my Instructor (not my TA) to determine what, if any, accommodations will be made.

2.2.1.5   Mark Appeals and Avenue to Learn Grades:

Specific protocols govern the mark appeal process for different components of evaluation in this course. I am aware that grades on homework tasks may not be appealed, and that appeals on grades on certain assignments and the mid-term must be made via the mark appeal process during assignment/test viewing periods. Once the assignment/viewing period has elapsed, I may no longer appeal the grade on that component of the course. My grade may go up or down as a result of any mark appeal.

My marks will be recorded on Avenue to Learn. It is my responsibility to check that all grades entered into Avenue to Learn are recorded properly. I must notify my T.A. about any errors with regards to how my mark was entered. I have until 48 hours prior to the final exam to discuss any mark issues.

2.2.1.6   Being a Student in Human Geography:

I am aware of the various course policies which govern student behaviour in class, the use of electronic devices in lecture and tutorial, the use of email (and proper email etiquette), and student use of Avenue to Learn. I realize that failure to abide by these regulations may result in sanctions such as being suspended from Avenue to Learn, asked to leave a classroom, etc.

2.2.1.7   Academic Integrity:

Academic Integrity is a very important issue at McMaster. It is my responsibility to understand what constitutes Academic Dishonesty. Among possible forms of academic dishonesty are: cheating on tests or exams by using unauthorized aids; inappropriately collaborating in group work; and plagiarism. For more information on what constitutes Academic Dishonesty, I should consult the University policy.

Furthermore, and of particular importance for this course I am aware that I must source ALL information that is not my own. If I submit an assignment with inadequate referencing I may face serious academic consequences (e.g. mark deductions, grade of zero, notation on my transcript, etc.).

I am aware of the importance of reading the Academic Integrity Slideshow. I am aware that I must read this material and complete the online quiz in order to receive any marks for assignments or tests.

2.2.2 Geographic Skills: Learning Modules:

Notes from 'Geographic Skills' Learning Modules: *What is a Map?*

Notes from 'Geographic Skills' Learning Modules (*Continued*): *Map Elements*

Notes from 'Geographic Skills' Learning Modules (*Continued*)**:** *Map Referencing Systems*

Notes from 'Geographic Skills' Learning Modules (*Continued*)**: *Contour Lines***

Notes from 'Geographic Skills' Learning Modules (*Continued***): *Map Projections***

Notes from 'Geographic Skills' Learning Modules (*Continued*)**:** *Fire Insurance Maps*

2.3 *Tutorial 2: Week of January 25-29, 2016*

- **Tutorial Location:**
  - o **Lloyd Reeds Map Collection (1st Floor, Mills Library)**

- Preparation:
  - o Make sure you know the location of the Map Collection
  - o View 'Course/Tutorial Organization & Course Policies' slideshow and complete the Student Responsibility Contract online quiz (Homework Task #1)
  - o View the 'Academic Integrity' slideshow and complete the online quiz (Homework Task #2)
  - o Complete 'Geographic Skills' online Learning Modules and pre-tutorial test

- Assignments:
  - o **Assignment #1 Introduced and Due (at the end of tutorial)**

- Tutorial Activities:
  - o Map Collection Introduction
  - o Assignment #1: Completion & Submission of Assignment during tutorial

- Courseware Readings:
  - o 'Geographic Skills' online Learning Modules
  - o Topographic Maps (chapter 7)

'Geographic Skills' Learning Modules: *There are questions on Assignment #1 that relate directly to the Geographic Skills online Learning Modules, so it would be wise to take notes while you view the material online and to review those notes prior to the beginning of tutorial. There is space to take notes at the end of the previous tutorial section (2.2.2).*

Pre-Tutorial Test: *It is not possible to complete the tutorial activities as planned without studying the online Learning Modules before your tutorial. As such, students are required to complete the Pre-Tutorial Test prior to the beginning of their tutorial (no less than 60 minutes before the beginning of the tutorial). The grade received on the Pre-Tutorial Test comprises part of the final grade received on Assignment #1.*

Map Collection Introduction: *At the beginning of the tutorial your TA will introduce you to the Map Collection and will explain how this tutorial will work. The materials used in this tutorial are of importance to completing Assignment #1, but many of the materials you are introduced to today will be of use for future assignments as well ...*

Rough Notes for Assignment #1:

Complete Assignment 1 – Your assignment <u>must</u> be submitted before the end of the tutorial

Homework Task #3: Research Skills

- One of the key skills to develop in university, especially early in your career, is how to navigate through the library catalogues to find academic literature. In order to assist you in this, we have developed a homework task which asks you to practice searching for, retrieving, and properly referencing academic materials you find via the library's catalogues.
    - ☐ First, review the online 'Information Literacy' modules (found on our Avenue to Learn site under 'Content' and 'Tutorial Materials')
    - ☐ Next, download Homework Task #3 from our Avenue to Learn site (under 'Content' and 'Homework Tasks')
    - ☐ Finally, complete Homework Task #3 and submit it to the appropriate Avenue to Learn drop-box (under 'Assessments') prior to the beginning of your next tutorial.

<u>Notes: Homework Tasks and Preparation for Next Tutorial:</u>

2.4 Assignment #1: Geographic Skills

Objective: The objectives of this assignment are three-fold:

1. Introduce students to the idea of 'thinking geographically'
2. Introduce students to one of the geographer's greatest tools: the map
3. Introduce students to the wide variety of maps and map tools available in the Map Collection

YOUR ASSIGNMENT WILL BE GIVEN TO YOU WHEN YOU ARRIVE AT THE MAP COLLECTION – PLEASE BE SURE TO ARRIVE ON TIME.

Group Work & Assistance: Your TA and the Map Collection staff are available, during your tutorial period to help you with your assignment. Your fellow students are also working on this assignment at the same time, and so helping each other figure things out is a good idea. In fact, some of this assignment is designed purposely to be collaborative so, on these sections we encourage you to work together. Keep in mind, however, that each student is to submit their own assignment.

Improper group collaboration is a form of Academic Dishonesty, and will not be tolerated.

Deadline: Assignment is due at the end of your tutorial

What to Submit:
☐ **All pages of this assignment**

Note: *This assignment is not a group assignment, although some tasks are designed to encourage collaboration. All answers to questions for this assignment must be your own.*

2.5 Tutorial 3: Week of February 1-5, 2016

- Preparation:
  - o Complete and submit Homework Task #3 (Research Skills)
  - o Read your assigned Wikipedia article
  - o Review the courseware readings (see below)

- Assignments:
  - o *None*

- Tutorial Activities:
  - o How to summarize detailed information succinctly: writing a précis
  - o The value of reflective thinking and writing: writing a reflection
  - o Thinking and writing critically
  - o Critical evaluation in-class activity
  - o Cultural regions: discussion and activity

- Courseware Readings:
  - o Writing Skills (chapter 3)

What is a Précis?

In-Class Précis Example:

What is the Purpose / Aim?

Who is the Audience?

What are the Major Themes?

Reflecting: What is the value of reflective thinking?

The typical components of a written reflection:

Descriptive Summary

A. Self-Reflection

B. Making Connections

C. Making Connections to Personal Experience

Other considerations when writing reflections:

Critically Evaluating Sources:

1. Accept the statement as fact?
2. Do some investigative work on your own?
3. Evaluate the credibility of the source?

While Critically Evaluating Sources, *Ask Yourself the Following Questions*:

1.

2.

3.

4.

5.

6.

In-Class Activity: Critically Evaluating Sources:

Source 1:

   Credible **Not Credible** **Unsure**

Source 2:

   Credible **Not Credible** **Unsure**

Source 3:

   Credible **Not Credible** **Unsure**

Source 4:

   Credible **Not Credible** **Unsure**

Group Activity: In-Class Critical Evaluation of Sources

- In small groups, based on the Wikipedia article you read, complete the in-class homework task provided by your TA (Homework Task #4). Submit this to your TA before the end of your tutorial.

Cultural Regions:

A cultural region is defined as:

A landscape (or cultural landscape) is defined as:

Thinking of Canada, how many cultural regions can you identify? Where are they?

How does your thinking of cultural regions change when we focus on the whole of North America rather than just Canada? How many cultural regions can you identify in North America?

Do any of your cultural regions remain the same when your spatial perspective changes from just Canada to the whole continent? How so?

Cultural regions are often associated with characteristic (iconic or symbolic) images of people, places, activities, etc. Thinking of the North American cultural regions, how would you characterize them – i.e. what are the common images associated with each of these North American cultural regions?

Group Activity: Cultural Regions

- In small groups, complete the in-class homework task (Homework Task #5) provided by your TA. Submit this to your TA before the end of your tutorial.

Homework Task #6: Spatial Analytical Tools - Reflection

- In Tutorial #1 (Introduction to Tutorials) you participated in an exercise using Google Earth as a way to navigate the world and explore various human landscapes. In Tutorial #2 (Geographic Skills & Map Library) you were introduced to, and engaged with, many different kinds of maps and map tools. Together, these two tutorial exercises have introduced you to a sampling of the many spatial analytical tools that are available. For this homework task we want you to reflect on the tools that you have seen so far, and think a little bit about the advantages and disadvantages of each.
    - ☐ Download Homework Task #6 from our Avenue to Learn site (under 'Content' and 'Homework Tasks')
    - ☐ Complete Homework Task #6 and submit it to the appropriate Avenue to Learn drop-box (under 'Assessments') prior to the beginning of your next tutorial.

Notes: Homework Tasks and Preparation for Next Tutorial:

2.6   Tutorial 4: Week of February 8-12, 2016

- Preparation:
  - o Complete and submit Homework Task #6 (Spatial Analytical Tools – Reflection)

- Assignments:
  - o *None*

- Tutorial Activities:
  - o Preparation for Health Geography Debate
  - o Population Video
  - o Population Issues: Group Activity

- Courseware Readings:
  - o Research Skills (chapter 5)

Introduction to Health-Care Debate:

- What is health-care? Who provides health-care (i.e. doctors, nurses, etc.)? What kinds of services constitute health-care (i.e. is massage therapy part of health-care? What about food banks?

- Is health-care delivered in the same way in all countries? What is the model of health-care in Canada? What about in other places?

- What works well in the Canadian health-care system? What does not work well in our system?

- Some people suggest that the Canadian health-care system should move more towards the American system (while many Americans think their health-care system should change to be more like ours). What is the American health-care system like?

- What is the best way to deliver health-care?

Health-Care Debate Format:

Questions to Consider when Researching the Debate Topic:

-
-
-
-

Health Geography Debate:

Group Topic: _____ **Side:** _____

Group Member Names: Email Address: Role in Debate:

-

-

-

-

-

-

-

-

Group Brainstorming

Homework Task #7: Health-Care Debate Research

- In order to properly prepare for your health-care debate you need to do some research on the issue. This research will be valuable to you during the debate.
    - ☐ Download **and print** Homework Task #7 from our Avenue to Learn site (under 'Content' and 'Homework Tasks')
    - ☐ Compile your research notes on the Homework Task #7 worksheet and bring to your next tutorial. You will be able to use your notes during the debate, but will then submit them to your TA at the end of the tutorial.

Video Notes: *World in the Balance*

Questions to consider:

- **India:**

- **Japan:**

- **United States:**

- **Africa:**

- **Overall:**

Notes:

Video Notes (*continued*):

Small Group Discussion Notes:

Homework Task #8: Population Issues - Reflection

- In light of your small group discussion about population issues, we want you to reflect on what you saw in the video and what you discussed in class.
    - ☐ Download Homework Task #8 from our Avenue to Learn site (under 'Content' and 'Homework Tasks')
    - ☐ Complete Homework Task #8 and submit it to the appropriate Avenue to Learn drop-box (under 'Assessments') prior to the beginning of your next tutorial.

Notes: Homework Tasks and Preparation for Next Tutorial:

2.7 Tutorial 5: Week of February 22-26, 2016

- Preparation:
  - o Conduct research on Health-Care: Complete Homework Task #7 (Health-Care Debate Research)
  - o Come prepared to participate in Health Geography Debate
  - o Complete and submit Homework Task #8 (Population Issues)

- Assignments:
  - o **Assignment #2 Introduced**

- Activity:
  - o Health Geography Debate

- Readings:
  - o *None*

Debate Logistics Notes:

Debate Notes:

Homework Task #9: Health-Care Debate - Reflection

- In light of your in-class debate and the research you conducted in preparation for it, we want you to reflect on the issue of a two-tiered health-care system.
  - ☐ Download Homework Task #9 from our Avenue to Learn site (under 'Content' and 'Homework Tasks')
  - ☐ Complete Homework Task #9 and submit it o the appropriate Avenue to Learn drop-box (under 'Assessments') prior to the beginning of your next tutorial.

Notes about Places and Culture:

Where does meaning come from?

-

-

e.g. places of worship vs. McDonald's

East Side Mario's

Placelessness

Introductory Notes about Assignment #2:

Basic Requirements of Assignment:

- **12 sites**

- **5 required sites:**

    ○

    ○

    ○

    ○

    ○

- **What constitutes a 'site':**

- **What is meant by a 'sub-area' within the neighbourhood:**

The Guidebook:

The Guidebook must include:

- ○
- ○
- ○
- ○
- ○
- ○
- ○
- ○

The Map:

The Map must include:

- ○
- ○
- ○
- ○
- ○
- ○

Research:

Fieldwork:

Group work:

My Partner:

Name: _____ **Email:** _____ **Phone:** _____

<u>Notes: Homework Tasks and Preparation for Next Tutorial:</u>

2.8 Assignment #2: Mapping a Local Neighbourhood – Dundas (Hamilton, Ontario)

Objective:
One of the unique aspects of geography, relative to other first year classes, is that it enables students to actually participate in the study of phenomena in the *field*. The purpose of this assignment is to provide you (with a partner) with the opportunity to do some traditional 'geographic' field work. You will use the local community (Hamilton, Ontario) as your field site. In addition to doing some field work, the assignment is designed to give you the chance to explore some methods of displaying geographic information through the use of maps. Furthermore, the assignment is designed to enable you to undertake some research as part of a group; group-work is a skill that you will need throughout your academic career as well as your post-academic career in all types of workplaces.

Introduction:
Fieldwork can take place in a wide variety of settings and can take on many different forms. In this assignment, your group will create an annotated digital map guidebook (basically like a walking tour guide) of the community known as Dundas in West Hamilton. Your guidebook will include maps, photographs, and commentary of the cultural (contemporary and historical) highlights of the neighbourhood.

Tasks:
1. Find a partner from within your tutorial.

2. Consult relevant materials (maps, books, etc.) in the Mills Library (Map Collection). These should help to give you some perspective, and to aid in your thinking of what to include in the guidebook. The Hamilton public library system has materials as well.

3. Design an annotated digital guidebook of the Dundas neighbourhood. For the purposes of this assignment, Dundas is defined by the area bounded by:
   - **West** – Market Street N. & S., **South** – Spencer Creek & Dundas Street, **East** – East Street N., and **North** – King Street E., West Street, Park Street, Cross Street, and Alma Street. *You will have access to a digital base map for reference and use.*
   - There are a number of features that you could include in the guidebook, but the following list indicates a few that MUST be included:

1. Dundas Town Hall	2. The Desjardins Canal	3. At least one church/place of worship
4. The Dundas Driving Park		
5. A 'sub-area' of the neighbourhood (your TA will explain what is meant by a sub-area)		

4. You will need to determine a starting and end point, as well as a **route**. You need to write a brief commentary about each of the important stops along the route (a minimum of 12 stops), describing the key features and characteristics of the buildings/locations as well as, perhaps where applicable, the history of the site.

5. You will need to produce a map of the tour route, indicating the locations of your key stops, key community information, as well as other marker locations which will enable a person using the guidebook, to not get lost along the way. Consult the map library staff, your textbook, your custom courseware for information regarding how to prepare maps and what to include on them.

6. You <u>will</u> need to visit each of the locations in order to get information for your commentary; to get illustrations for your write-up (i.e. sketches, photographs, etc.); to determine the length of time required to spend at and between each site on the route; as well as directions for getting from site to site. As you visit each site, and the neighbourhood more generally, you will record your observations as field notes. Your field notes are to be submitted (as part of your assignment), and **must** be hand-written; we want your raw (unrevised) thoughts from the field, not polished analyses from after the fact.

7. **It is absolutely imperative that you do not interview people while out in the field.** This assignment requires you to do research (from library and archival sources) and field observations, it does not require you to speak to residents or business owners. Please do not go **into** any of the sites.

The Guidebook:
The guidebook (between 2500-3500 words) should provide detailed information about a) each of the sites and their **characteristic features, history, architecture, changing uses, etc.**, and b) a description of how to traverse from one site to the next.

Your guidebook should also have an introductory section which provides the reader with an overall assessment of the character of the present-day Dundas neighbourhood as well as the community's past. Illustrations may be included, and will not count towards the word-limit.

You must also include a list of references page (will not count towards the word limit). Remember, when using other sources you MUST reference them.

The Map:
You must prepare a detailed map showing the entire Dundas neighbourhood including the 12 or more sites you chose to highlight in your guidebook; digital base maps will be available. In addition to the spatial extent of the community (i.e. the boundaries) and the key features you discuss in the guidebook, your map should indicate the basic street pattern and areas of specific land use (i.e. parks, schools, residential areas, etc.).

Additional assignment <u>requirements</u> will be provided by your TA in tutorial.

●──●

Deadline: Your assignment is to be submitted to the appropriate Avenue to Learn drop-box prior to the beginning of your tutorial during the week of March 28-April 1, 2016.

What to submit:
☐ **A Digital Guidebook: this includes a title page (see note below), an annotated map of the Dundas neighbourhood, between 2500-3500 words of written text, plus any illustrations you feel are appropriate, including one photograph (minimum) of you are your partner together in the field; all material which is not from your own observations must be properly cited and you must include a proper reference list.**
☐ **Hand-Written Field Notes: a full set of hand-written field notes must be submitted by the group (this includes observations and sketch maps for all 12 sites). Each student will be responsible for producing approximately 6 of these.**

Note: You must also clearly state, on the cover page of your assignment, that both members have read and abided by the Guidelines for Student Fieldwork. By placing your names beneath this statement, you are effectively signing it.

2.8.1   Assignment #2 - Guidelines for Student Fieldwork

General and Course-Specific Guidelines:

Teamwork: You are **required** to conduct your research in pairs.

Timing: Find a convenient time to complete your fieldwork. You may go either during the week or at the weekend. You are strongly encouraged to complete your fieldwork in the daytime.

It is your responsibility to make sure that you go and do the fieldwork components of the assignment when the weather is suitable. There will be no extensions due to inclement weather, so make sure you do not leave the fieldwork component to the last minute.

Etiquette: You are going out to observe the local community and to undertake traditional field observation methods. As a result you will become part of that environment. How you behave is therefore critically important. Conduct your fieldwork in a manner that is respectful of the people around you. You are representing McMaster University when you are doing your fieldwork, and so please make sure that you are on your best behaviour and are professional at all times. Please respect private property, commercial businesses and public spaces. You are not to interfere with the everyday activities of your study area.

Do **NOT** actively seek out conversations with people; the fieldwork component of this assignment does NOT require that you interview people. In fact, *under no circumstances are you to bother people at these sites. It is not our intention for you to speak to local merchants or people at the various sites; you are to do your own research before or after your visit.* Do not ask people what the history of a building is, etc. It is not their job to tell you this, and this is not the intent of the fieldwork that you are doing.

If anyone does ask what you are doing, explain the assignment to them. If they want more information, please refer them to Dr. Mercier at 905 525-9140, Ext.27597.

Travel: The neighbourhood of study is a short walk, bus ride or drive from the McMaster campus. Do NOT attempt to do your fieldwork in a vehicle; this is intended to be a 'walking tour'. We anticipate the field visits will take between two and five hours, with some additional travel-time.

Refusal of unsafe work: Each student has the legal right to refuse, at any time, to participate in any activity that he/she feels may endanger his/her health or safety or the safety of another person.

You must clearly state, on the cover page of your assignment, that both members have read and abided by the Guidelines for Student Fieldwork. By placing your names beneath this statement, you are effectively signing it.

2.9 *Tutorial 6: Week of February 29-March 4, 2016*

- Preparation:
  - o Complete and submit Homework Task #8 (Health-Care Debate - Reflection)
  - o Read Chapter 6 (Fieldwork) in your courseware
  - o Bring your courseware, a pencil, and a clipboard to tutorial

- Assignments:
  - o *None*

- Tutorial Activities:
  - o Hamilton: Discussion
  - o Introduction to Fieldwork
  - o Fieldwork Activity

- Courseware Readings:
  - o Fieldwork (chapter 6)

Hamilton Residents vs. Non-Residents:

	Positive Aspects	Negative Aspects
1.		
2.		
3.		
4.		
5.		
6.		
7.		
8.		
9.		
10.		

Hamilton Class Discussion Notes:

Hamilton's Image Discussion Notes: *Perception vs. Reality*

Hamilton's Image Discussion Notes: *Past vs. Present vs. Future*

Consider Hamilton's current employment structure: the leading employment sector today is health-care and education NOT industrial production.

So, why does Hamilton's industrial history continue to over-shadow this?

Hamilton's Image Video Notes: *The Ambitious City*

Consider why Hamilton is considered the 'Ambitious City'.

Homework Task #10: Hamilton's Image - Reflection

- In light of your in-class discussions and the 'Ambitious City' video, we want you to reflect on Hamilton's image.
  - ☐ First, begin by reading the Rosie Dimanno article for yourself, as well as a counterpoint article by Matthew Van Dongen. Both articles can be found on our Avenue to Learn site (under 'Content' and 'Tutorial Materials').
  - ☐ Next, download Homework Task #10 from our Avenue to Learn site (under 'Content' and 'Homework Tasks')
  - ☐ Finally, complete Homework Task #10 and submit it to the appropriate Avenue to Learn drop-box (under 'Assessments') prior to the beginning of your next tutorial.

Notes on Doing <u>Field</u>work:

What is fieldwork?

Why do we do fieldwork?

What kinds of things do we do when we do fieldwork?

Field Notes take two primary forms:

1. **Observations**

   •

   •

   •

   •

2. **Sketch Maps**

In-Class Activity: Fieldwork on Campus

- Individually, complete the in-class activity (Homework Task #11) provided by your TA. Submit this to your TA before the end of your tutorial.

Notes: Homework Tasks and Preparation for Next Tutorial:

2.10 Tutorial 7: Week of March 7-11, 2016

- Preparation:
  o Complete Homework Task #10 (Hamilton Image - Reflection)
  o Conduct Fieldwork for Assignment #2

- Assignments:
  o *None*

- Activities:
  o Video: Hamilton
  o Group Work Meeting Time for Assignment #2 – Visit the Map Collection

- Courseware Readings:
  o *None*

Hamilton History: Discussion

Can you identify any influential people (past or present) from Hamilton, and their legacy to the city?

What industry is most closely linked to Hamilton's history and when did this begin?

What are some of the most important events in Hamilton's history?

Video: *Where the Rubber Meets the Road* – **Notes:**

Video: *Where the Rubber Meets the Road* – Notes (*continued*):

Themes of the video:

-

-

-

Consider how the information in the video might be useful for Assignment #2 ...

Notes on Assignment #2 Library Resources:

Notes: Homework Tasks and Preparation for Next Tutorial:

2.11 Tutorial 8: Week of March 14-18, 2016

- Preparation:
    - Conduct research for Assignment #2

- Assignments:
    - *None*

- Tutorial Activities:
    - Cultural Landscapes
    - Seven Wonders of the World Discussion
    - Cultural Landscapes Game
    - Assignment #2 Revisited

- Courseware Readings:
    - *None*

Cultural Landscapes:

Key Elements of Cultural Landscapes:

1.

2.

3.

Each culture imprints itself on the landscape in different ways, and so from one place to another we see different cultural landscapes

Cultural landscape (definition):

The cultural landscape is fashioned from a natural landscape by a cultural group. Culture is the agent, the natural are the medium, the cultural landscape is the result"
- Carl Sauer, 1925

Landscape as a Human System

Landscapes are comprised of cultural artefacts:

    1. Functional e.g.

    2. Symbolic e.g.

Sense of Place (definition):

Examples:

Cultural Landscape Discussion:

What are some other examples of places with collective meaning or significance?

Seven Wonders of the Ancient World:

Notes:

1.

2.

3.

4.

5.

6.

7.

Seven Wonders of the Modern World:

Notes:

1.

2.

3.

4.

5.

6.

7.

What other one should be on this list?

Canada's Seven Wonders:

Group Discussion Notes:

Our List:

1.

2.

3.

4.

5.

6.

7.

Cultural Landscapes Trivia Game:

Cultural Landscape:	Cultural Landscape:
1.	11.
2.	12.
3.	13.
4.	14.
5.	15.
6.	16.
7.	17.
8.	18.
9.	19.
10.	20.

Note: In addition to listing the 20 cultural landscapes in the table above, plot each location on the map (next page)

Of the 20 cultural landscapes, my 'top 5' places to visit are:

1.

2.

3.

4.

5.

Cultural Landscapes Trivia Game (*continued*):

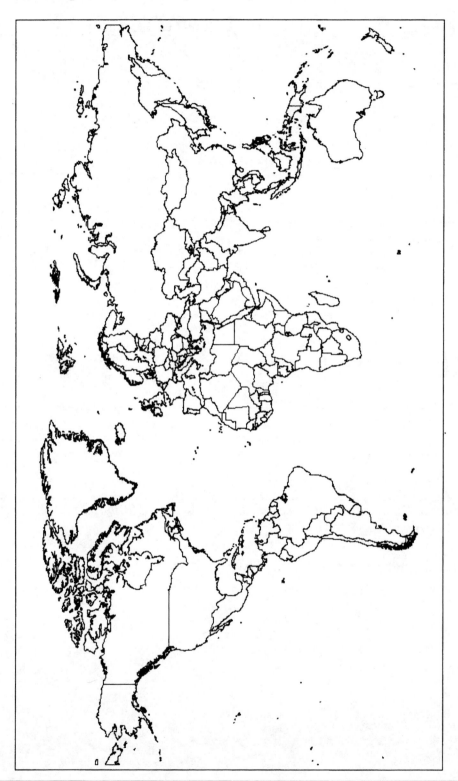

Notes for Assignment #2:

Geographic Information Systems (GIS): *Homework Task #12*

- **Earlier this semester, we had a special guest lecturer (Pat DeLuca). Pat introduced us to GIS (Geographical Information Systems) as a convenient and powerful tool to represent and understand spatial data and phenomena. Your homework is to produce your very own GIS map(s) and answer a few simple questions about them.**
  - ☐ First, download the step-by-step instructions on how to produce a simple map. The instructions can be found on our Avenue to Learn site under 'Content' and 'Tutorial Materials'.
  - ☐ Next, download Homework Task #12 from our Avenue to Learn site (under 'Content' and 'Homework Tasks')
  - ☐ Finally, complete Homework Task #12 and submit it (along with your maps) to the appropriate Avenue to Learn drop-box (under 'Assessments') prior to the beginning of your FINAL tutorial (i.e. two weeks).

Notes: Homework Tasks and Preparation for Next Tutorial:

2.12   Tutorial 9: Week of March 21-25, 2016

- <u>Preparation</u>:
  - o Bring any final questions you have regarding Assignment #2
  - o Bring any questions you have regarding Homework Task #12 (due in Tutorial #10)

- <u>Assignments</u>:
  - o *None*

- <u>Activities</u>:
  - o Group Discussion – Culture
  - o Group Discussion – Political Hot Topics
  - o Group Meeting Time - Assignment #2

- <u>Courseware Readings</u>:
  - o *None*

Discussion about Spatial Variations in Culture:

Our world is divided especially because of spatial variations in culture.

Small Group Discussion - Notes

1. **Language or religion, which is the most important component of culture?**

Small Group Discussion – Notes (*Continued*)

2. **Cultural Globalization is in everyone's best interest because local variations in culture are responsible for barriers and conflicts between peoples**

Class Discussion: Additional Notes

Spatial Variations in Culture:

Is there any truth to the idea that Canada and the United States have <u>different</u> cultures?

- **What perceptions do Canadians have about Americans and American culture?**

- **What perceptions do Americans have about Canadians and Canadian culture?**

- **Do these perceptions intersect (match) or are they different? Why?**

Tom Brokaw:

Political 'Hot Topics' Small Group Discussion:

- In small groups, complete the in-class homework task (Homework Task #13) provided by your TA. Submit this to your TA before the end of your tutorial.

Final Reminders for Assignment #2:

Notes: Homework Tasks and Preparation for Next Tutorial:

2.13   *Tutorial 10: Week of March 28-April 1, 2016*

- Preparation:
  - o Complete and submit Homework Task #12 (GIS)
  - o Complete and submit Assignment #2

- Assignments:
  - o **Assignment #2 Due**

- Activities:
  - o Course Evaluations
  - o How Well Do You Know Your World (re-visited)
  - o Exam Information, Preparation & Review
  - o Study Tips
  - o. Course Wrap-Up Tasks

- Courseware Readings:
  - o *None*

How Well Do You Know Your World (Re-Visited): Small Group & Large Group Activity

In small groups, using the map provided by your TA, locate the following places. When you take them up as a class, you can plot them on the map (next page) for your own future reference (***exam hint***).

- Locate Hamilton, Ontario
- Locate and **shade** the FIVE most populous countries
- Locate and label the LARGEST city in the United States
- Identify the largest country in the former USSR/Soviet Union
- Locate the Sahara Desert
- Locate and label the following FIVE cultural landscapes:
  - o Christ the Redeemer
  - o Sydney Opera House
  - o The Taj Mahal
  - o The Coliseum
  - o Pyramids of Giza
- Locate the country that hosted the most recent World Cup of soccer (men)

How Well Do You Know Your World (Re-Visited):

In this course we have talked about many global issues. Geography is essential to your understanding of these issues.

- Is there anything unique or interesting about your group's map?

- How has your knowledge of the world changed, in light of what you have learned in this course?

- Do you have a better understanding of where things are and how things and places are interconnected?

Geography is NOT simply about memorizing place names and spatial facts, but is about knowing and understanding both the global and local significance of a variety of issues. Part of this understanding is what is known as "geographical understanding".

When we know *what is where*, *why there*, and *why we care*, we have a true geographical understanding

Exam Information:

Exam Details:

Date: _____

Time: _____

Duration: _____

Weighting: _____

MY Location: _____ .

What I need to bring:

Exam Format:

Exam Preparation Exercise: Notes

Exam Review (key terms & concepts, definitions, types of questions, etc.):

Study Tips:

- **Sleep**

- **Food**

- **Studying**

- **Organization**

- **Active Studying**

- **Avoid Cramming**

Final Notes re. Course Grades, etc.:

3.0 Writing Skills & Referencing

3.1 Introduction to Writing Skills

> **Recommended Writing Guide:**
> *Making Sense – A Student's Guide to Research and Writing* by Margot Northey, Dianne Draper and David Knight (2015). This book is widely available at the Campus Store (bookstore) and through online booksellers. For the full reference for this book, see Chapter 8.

Writing involves much more than simply writing out ideas on paper or computer. Planning, researching, drafting and proofing are among the steps required to reach a well written final product. Writing is a skill which takes time and practice to do well. A good writing guide should be considered essential by all students. Scientific inquiry is undertaken to learn new information and dissemination of learning is only possible through clearly written work. Although often undervalued, all science students should strive to learn the skills of writing.

This chapter will guide you through the basics of writing a précis and a research paper. The required referencing style for most human geography courses is also included here.

3.2 Writing a Précis

Students in an introductory writing class were asked to write a 100-word condensation of a 3500-word essay. Impossible? No, but difficult and exacting.

A précis is a condensation *in your own words* of a short work; an article, an essay, or perhaps a chapter in a book. The technique of précis writing requires that you read closely and write precisely. Writing a précis is excellent practice for taking notes (especially for the research paper) and for developing reading and writing skills. Here are the guidelines for précis writing:

1. Highlight the most important ideas and omit the specifics. Record the bare bones of the article, leaving out all subordinate ideas and modifiers.
2. Observe accurately. Report exactly what you read *in the order in which it is presented*. *Do not inject your own opinion*. This includes *not* writing in first person.
3. Make every word count. Eliminate all unnecessary words from your writing. Keep to the bare essentials.
4. Observe the word limit given by your Instructor.

> A common mistake made by students writing a précis is writing in first person. This should not be done. Keep your précis impersonal and do not inject your own opinion.

3.3   *Writing a Reflection*

In many classes students are asked to reflect on something that they have read, or something that they have discussed in small or large groups, or something that they have done as part of a course-related task or experiential activity. Reflecting is one of the most important components of the learning process, as it helps to make what students have learned (or are learning) more concrete. The way that learning becomes more concrete through reflection is via transforming abstract concepts or theories into ones that are tied to individual experience. And it is this individual experience that students tend to remember long term.

Fundamentally, through writing reflections we aim to ask ourselves questions about how our understanding of an issue or concept has changed, and to make connections to our personal experiences and/or what we have learned elsewhere via other courses, etc.

The typical components of a written reflection include:·
- A short (paragraph or two) descriptive summary (or précis) of the issue as outlined via the reading, discussion, or activity; and

- A short (paragraph or two) written assessment of one, two or all three of the following:
  A. Self-reflection about whether your knowledge or understanding of the issue has been impacted (changed) as a result of having done the reading, participated in the discussion, or completed an activity
    - You might want to ask yourself the following types of questions:
      - Has the reading/discussion/activity changed my way of thinking about this issue?
      - Did the reading/discussion/activity conflict with and/or build on what I thought previously?
      - What, specifically, about the reading/discussion/activity changed my thinking about this issue?

  B. Making connections between your reading/discussion/activity and what you have learned elsewhere
    - How do the ideas expressed in the reading/discussion/experience mesh with, or conflict with, what I have learned about elsewhere?
    - What, specifically, about the reading/discussion/activity supports, contradicts, or challenges what I have learned elsewhere?

  C. Making connections between your reading/discussion/activity and your own personal experiences
    - How do the ideas expressed in the reading/discussion/experience mesh with, or conflict with, my own personal experiences?
    - What, specifically, about the reading/discussion/activity supports, contradicts, or challenges my own personal experiences with this issue?

The art of reflection necessitates the asking of questions about what we know about something, what our biases are, and what we have learned. In addition, reflective thinking requires us to be open to admitting that our previous assumptions may have been incorrect, or that our opinion may have been misinformed. This does not mean that our initial assumptions are always incorrect, but rather that we need to be open to the idea that that may be the case, and that it is okay to admit that when it is true.

Reflections are typically short (~300-600 words; one to two pages), but you should be sure to check what the specific guidelines are for each reflection you write. Reflections are also intended to be both personal and subjective, meaning that the use of personal pronouns (i.e. "I") are acceptable. But, at the same time, this is an academic exercise not a personal journal/diary entry, and so the writing must maintain an academic tone, and must be coherent and logically organized. As such, you need to use full sentences, complete paragraphs, proper punctuation, and must make wise grammar and word choices (i.e. no slang, etc.).

Evaluating reflections is a difficult task, as it is pretty difficult to argue that one's self-reflection is wrong. However, like most written work, it is relatively straight-forward to identify students who have put more thought into their self-reflection, or who have made more meaningful connections to either personal experiences or things they have learned in other courses. Further, some students are better able to concisely describe the issue portrayed through the reading, discussion or activity. As such, while to a certain degree reflections in this course will be marked on a completion basis, there is ample opportunity to differentiate written reflections by the quality of the written description and the analytical depth of either the self-reflection or the connections made.

3.4   Writing Research Papers

1.   When choosing a topic, start with a general idea. Use preliminary research to refine your topic. Make sure your topic a) can be researched effectively, b) interests you, and c) relates to the course material.

2.   The title should always reflect the main purpose and objectives of the report. The Title should appear on the front page of your report along with all other required information (e.g. name, student number, date and course code).

3.   A research paper consists of 3 parts:
    1.   *Introduction:* outline of the topic to be addressed, necessary background information, the objectives of the research, your thesis. You 'set the scene' for the reader. Try to make it interesting, an introduction should engage the reader.
    2.   *Discussion:* address the topic in more detail, divide it into different sections (using subheadings) and discuss the main ideas. Introduce ideas, hypotheses, opinions, etc. Make sure to stay focussed, everything you discuss should relate to your topic.
    3.   *Conclusion:* reminder of the most important points of the research. Do not just regurgitate points from your introduction. Do not introduce any new ideas in this section.

4. Organize your thoughts before writing them down. Make a concise outline of the points you want to address and what you want to say about each one. Set up the structure of your paper; make sure your paper follows a logical progression of ideas. Follow your outline when writing, and be conscious of any word or page limit set out by your Instructor.

5. Use as many diagrams and figures as possible - a picture is worth a thousand words! Always refer to your figure in the text; e.g. "Figure 1 illustrates the location of earthquake epicentres..." or "Earthquakes occur most commonly at plate boundaries (Fig. 1). Each figure should have a caption below it stating what it shows and where it is taken from (unless you made the figure yourself); e.g. "Figure 1: World earthquake epicentres (Montgomery, 1989)". Note that everything is either a figure or a table - e.g. graphs, figures, maps, illustrations and diagrams should all be referred to as figures.

6. Make sure that you provide supporting evidence for your statements. For example, if you say world hunger is on the increase, you must provide evidence to show that this is true.

7. Always reference your sources of information! Give credit where credit is due, otherwise you may be accused of plagiarism.

8. Never write in first person (i.e. I or we). Keep the report impersonal and formal.

9. Pay attention to grammar and spelling. Use paragraphs each time you start a new idea within the same section. Do not use contractions such as don't or can't. Avoid extensive use of the passive voice. Writing should be fluent, with transitions between paragraphs.

10. Always proofread your work before handing it in. Better still, have one of your friends read it over as they can often find errors you missed and can comment on the organisation and clarity of your report.

11. Last but not least: make your report look neat and well organized; it can save you marks.

3.5   Referencing

3.5.1   CITING A REFERENCE IN THE TEXT: CITATIONS

Any idea or information you use in a paper or report that is not your own must be referenced within the body of the text. This is done by giving the author (or authors) and the date of publishing in parentheses in, or at the end of, any sentence that needs to be referenced. This style of referencing is common in the social sciences and is referred to as parenthetical referencing or APA style. For example,

There are many different methods of administrating questionnaires (Smith, 2007).

or

Smith (2007) identifies a number of different methods of administering questionnaires.

If a number of articles are being referenced to support an idea, they are all enclosed in the same bracket, in alphabetical order and separated by a semi-colon (;). If there are two authors for an article or book, list both separated by an ampersand (&); if there are three or more authors, list the first and add *'et al.'* (short form of *et alia*, Latin for 'and others'). For example,

> Geography is one of the most interesting courses that can be taken at McMaster University (Flanders, 1972; Gumbel & Smithers, 1985; Simpson et al., 1988).

When quoting the authors directly, or providing a specific 'fact' you must also provide the page number (on which the quote or fact appears in the source). For example,

> "What is the 'geographical imagination'? Simply put, it is appreciation of the relevance of space and place to all aspects of human geography" (Norton, 2007, p. 607).

or

> Canada's population, according to the most recent Census, is 34 million (Norton, 2009, p. 348).

Many sources today are available in electronic format (either instead of, or in addition to, traditional hard-copy paper formats). The style of in-text (parenthetical) referencing for electronic sources is the same as for traditional sources. The in-text citation should give the author's name (which may be an institution, organization, government agency, etc.) and the year in which the reference was created or last amended (most websites include a 'Page Last Updated on ..." towards the bottom of the webpage). If there is no obvious date of authorship then you should record this as 'undated'. For example,

> Obtaining accurate estimates of the total number of refugees leaving Afghanistan between 1990-1999 are complicated by the fact that the country has not conducted a recent Census (United Nations, 2004).

or

> The 'troubles' in Ireland can be traced back as far as the infamous Battle of the Boyne, if not earlier (Political Watchdog, Undated).

Full bibliographic information about each source (traditional or electronic) is then given in a reference list at the end of your paper or report. This list is entitled *Reference List* or *Works Cited*. Only items that were directly **referred to** in the text of the report should be included.

Warning:

Do not treat referencing as an after thought. Academic dishonesty is a very serious offence and is not treated lightly by the School of Geography and Earth Sciences. Make sure you read this section carefully and reference all of the sources you use for any work you submit. The Senate Policy on Academic Integrity is available online:

http://www. mcmaster.ca/senate/academic/ac_integrity.htm

3.5.2   CREATING A REFERENCE LIST:

A reference list is a list of works organized alphabetically according to the last name of the first author of a work. This list provides full information about any referenced source. It only includes materials that are actually referenced in the report.

To create a reference list, follow these guidelines:
- Alphabetize *all* sources by using the last name of the first author.
- If your list includes single-author works by people with the same last name, alphabetize using the authors' first initial (and then second initial, where necessary).
- If you have works by one author and other works that this same author has co-authored, list the author's works by him/her alone, then list the works that he/she has co-authored.
- If you have a series of works by the same author(s), list the works in chronological order according to the publication date, starting with the oldest to the most recent. If an author has two or more papers published in the same year you can add a,b,c etc. after the date of publication e.g. Mercier, M. (1998a).

3.5.3   REFERENCING DIFFERENT TYPES OF PUBLICATIONS:
Traditional Sources

3.5.3.1   BOOK – SINGLE AUTHOR

For the title of a book, it is customary to capitalize the first word, as well as the first word following a colon, and any proper or place names.

Harris, R. (1996). *Unplanned suburbs: Toronto's American tragedy*. Baltimore: Johns Hopkins University Press.

3.5.3.2   BOOK – TWO AUTHORS

Knox, P., & Pinch, S. (2006). *Urban social geography: An introduction*. Toronto: Pearson-Prentice Hall.

3.5.3.3   BOOK – MORE THAN TWO AUTHORS

Kuby, M., Harner, J., & Gober, P. (2007). *Human geography in action*. Hoboken, NJ: John Wiley & Sons.

3.5.3.4   BOOK WITH CORPORATE OR GOVERNMENT AUTHOR

If responsibility for the contents of the book is taken by an agency, corporation, or institute, use the name of this group as the author. Alphabetize according to the first word in the name (disregarding *the, an,* and *a*). Spell out the full name of the group. Give the name of the parent body before listing subdivisions of the organization.

Environment Canada. (1966). *The state of Canada's environment*. Ottawa: Queen's Printer.

3.5.3.5 BOOK – EDITION OTHER THAN THE ORIGINAL

Norton, W. (2009). *Human geography* (7th ed.). Toronto: Oxford University Press.

3.5.3.6 BOOK – WITH EDITOR RATHER THAN AUTHOR

Very often in the social sciences, books are collections of articles or chapters written by a number of different people and gathered together by an editor. These books will use the editor (indicated by Ed., or Eds. for more than one) as the author.

Bourne, L., & Ley, D. (Eds.) (1993). *The changing social geography of Canadian cities*. Montreal: McGill-Queen's University Press.

3.5.3.7 WORK IN AN EDITED VOLUME

For an article or chapter appearing in an edited volume, you need to specify the specific location in the book. The numbers at the end of the reference are the inclusive page numbers of the article or chapter cited. The title of the article/chapter is listed after the author (and date) and before the information about the book or volume in which it is found. The title of the article/chapter follows the same rules about capitalization as book titles (see 3.4.3.1).

Moore, E. & Rosenberg, M. (1993). Migration, mobility and population redistribution. In L. Bourne & D. Ley (Eds.) *The changing social geography of Canadian cities* (pp. 121-137). Montreal: McGill-Queen's University Press.

3.5.3.8 ARTICLE IN A SCHOLARLY JOURNAL

The format for a reference to an article in a journal is largely the same as a chapter in an edited book (see 3.4.3.7 above). The numbers after the journal title (e.g. 35:4) are the volume and issue numbers; it is customary to include both the volume and the issue number together, separated by a colon only when the entire volume is not paginated continuously. The numbers at the end of the reference are the inclusive page numbers of the article. In contrast to book titles, it is customary to capitalize all words in the **title of the journal**.

Lewis, R. (2001). A city transformed: Manufacturing districts and suburban growth in Montreal, 1850-1941. *Journal of Historical Geography, 27*, 20-35.

Be aware that most scholarly journals today are available in both print and electronic (online) formats. These should be regarded as traditional sources and not electronic ones.

3.5.3.9 ARTICLE IN A MAGAZINE

Since general-interest periodicals (magazines), which are usually published weekly or monthly, normally begin each issue with page 1, you must always give the specific date or month of the issue you are referring to.

Johnson, J. (2009). Plugging into the sun. *National Geographic, Sept.* 28-53.

If the article does not have an author, begin your entry with the title. Alphabetize by using their first main word, disregarding *the, an,* and *a.* For your parenthetical citation, shorten the title by using the first word or two; if, for example, the article above had no author, your citation would be (Plugging, 2009).

3.5.3.10   ARTICLE IN A NEWSPAPER

There is no specific form for newspaper articles, as they rarely appear in scientific papers. You could modify the form for magazines if you need to reference such a source.

Shaffer, R. (1983). Digital audio already altering recording industry's practices. *The Wall Street Journal, April 29*, 27.

If the article does not have an author, begin your entry with the title. Alphabetize by using the first main word, disregarding *the, an,* and *a.* For your parenthetical citation, shorten the title by using the first word or two of the article title e.g. (Digital Audio, 1983).

3.5.3.11   REFERENCING A LECTURE

To reference a lecture, give the name of the lecturer, the title of the lecture, the course and where and when it was held.

Mercier, Michael. (2010). The geography of language. GEOG 1HA3, McMaster University, November 30.

3.5.4   REFERENCING DIFFERENT TYPES OF PUBLICATIONS: Electronic Sources

3.5.4.1   WORLD WIDE WEB, HOME PAGE

References to original content from online sources should contain the following key information: the author of the content, the date of publication or last update, the title of the page, the name of the organization/individual that maintains the site, the date of access or retrieval, and the URL.

Geological Survey of Canada. (2004, February). *A map of Canada's earth materials.* Retrieved December 1, 2006, from http://canada.geoscape.nrcan.gc.ca/geo_can_t2/index_e.aspx.

If the date of internet publication is not given on the site, reference the date it was accessed at the beginning of the citation. As many sites may be organizations or institutions, you may give a short form of the author name in your parenthetical citation in the text; e.g. (GSC, 2004) instead of (Geological Survey of Canada, 2004).

When referencing any other resources from the Internet such as a book, encyclopaedia, magazine article, etc. follow the same basic format as if they were traditional sources (see section 3.4.3).

Warning: Be aware of fraudulent information on the Internet. Anyone can put information on the internet under an alias name. Make sure you critically investigate the sources of the information from the Internet that you are using for your research paper.

In addition, be aware that most scholarly journals today are available in both print and electronic (online) formats. These should <u>not</u> be regarded as online sources (websites), but rather as traditional sources and should be referenced accordingly (see section 3.4.3).

3.5.4.2   REFERENCING A PERSONAL ELECTRONIC COMMUNCATION (E-MAIL)

While uncommon, it may occasionally be necessary to reference information provided to you via personal communication, i.e. an email. References to email or other forms of personal communication should contain the following key information: the author (sender) of the content, the email (or other) address of the author, the date of receipt, the subject of the message.

Omar, B. (<u>bomar@yahoo.ca</u>). (1996, June 5). *Excellent web sites for geographers.*

3.5.5   REFERENCING OTHER TYPES OF SOURCES

Referencing Information Sources Found in Urban Landscapes

In certain instances the field itself provides specific information which can/should be recorded in your field notes and cited in your text. When you use this information in an essay, assignment, or research paper, you must provide the reader with the source of this information just as you would if you were citing a book or journal article. Two sources frequently encountered in urban landscapes are plaques and cornerstones.

<u>Plaques:</u>

When citing information found on a plaque, you should indicate the following:
- The location of the plaque; and
- The government body or agency responsible for erecting the plaque (e.g. federal, provincial or municipal government, or a non-governmental community agency)

Example:
"St. Paul's Presbyterian Church is designated as a National Historic Site. According to the plaque (located at the front of the building on James St. South) erected by the National Historic Sites and Monuments Board of Canada, St. Paul's was designed by the architect William Thomas and construction was completed in 1857."

<u>Cornerstones:</u>

Occasionally, buildings themselves provide information through inscriptions on cornerstones. When citing information found on a cornerstone, you should indicate the following:
- The name, address, and/or location of the building; and
- The location <u>on</u> the building of the cornerstone

Example:
"The cornerstone of McMaster's University Hall is located to the left of the archway under the building's tower. The cornerstone was laid by Viscount Wellington, the Governor General of Canada on October 8, 1929 and signifies the date of construction of the building."

3.5.6   THE FINAL REFERENCE LIST

Your reference list will be typed on a separate sheet or sheets of paper, using the same margins as those in the body of your paper. Number the pages consecutively with other pages in the text, remembering that any notes and/or appendices will be placed between the body of the paper and the reference list. You may head the list "References". Centre the heading at the top of the page, leaving at least one line of space between it and the first entry on the list. The first line of each entry will be flush with the left-hand margin; other lines of individual entries are indented five spaces.

3.6   Preparing an Annotated Bibliography

What is an annotated bibliography?
Annotated bibliographies are used to evaluate the credibility of a source. They include the components of a traditional bibliography, including citations for sources such as books, journals, articles, documents etc., in addition to a short description, usually 150 words, which assesses how significant, accurate and eminent the source is.

What is an annotation?
Annotations are commonly confused with abstracts. Annotations critically evaluate the information contained in a book, document, article etc. They interpret the main ideas of the information presented by the source, while determining related importance and validity. Abstracts provide summaries of scholarly journal articles and indexes. Abstracts provide only a summary, whereas annotations provide a summary with a critical perspective that evaluates the source.

The Process
The process of preparing an annotated bibliography includes the following steps:
- First obtain books, articles, documents etc. that contain pertinent information that is related to your research topic. Review these sources to ensure that a wide spectrum of information has been collected.
- Secondly, cite each source appropriately (refer to pages 41-49 in the Handbook for the Earth and Environmental Sciences Student)

- Configure an annotation for each cited source and include the following:
    - summary of the information presented on the related topic
    - assess the author/authority of the source
    - note the intended audience
    - comment on the quality of the information presented
    - explain the relevance of this work to your research topic

Annotated Bibliography: Example

Goldschneider, F., Waite, L., & Witsberger, C. (1986). Nonfamily living and the erosion of traditional family orientations among young adults. *American Sociological Review, 51*, 541-554.

The authors, researchers at the Rand Corporation and Brown University, use data from the National Longitudinal Surveys of Young Women and Young Men to test their hypothesis that nonfamily living by young adults alters their attitudes, values, plans, and expectations, moving them away from their belief in traditional sex roles. They find their hypothesis strongly supported in young females, while the effects were fewer in studies of young males. Increasing the time away from parents before marrying increased individualism, self-sufficiency, and changes in attitudes about families. In contrast, an earlier study by Williams cited below shows no significant gender differences in sex role attitudes as a result of nonfamily living.

4.0   Group Work Skills

4.1   Introduction to Group Work

Most 'work', whether it is for government, industry or academic purposes, involves interdisciplinary co-operation between a number of individuals and it is important that you gain experience of group work. It is not a simple task to work effectively as part of a group or team; it involves the development of effective group working skills.

In all group-work environments it is imperative to understand that all members of the group are ultimately responsible for the end product. Remember, if your name is on it, you are responsible for its content.

Group work is not simply about a number of individuals putting their work together; group work is about much more than that. Group work is really about collaboration and providing a better product than individuals could produce on their own. Collaboration means working together (not apart); collaboration means working as a team (not as individuals); and collaboration means working better (not less). As such, do not think about group work as a way to 'split up the work', but rather think of it as a way to collaborate with your peers, and to produce a truly exceptional piece of work; something that you could not have produced alone.

In this section some of the fundamentals of effective group working will be discussed. However, nothing will help you more than experience and practice!! A valuable source is Don Woods' book "How to gain the most from Problem-Based Learning' available in the bookstore (these notes have been modified from Woods' book).

4.2   Characteristics of Groups

- A group works best with 3 or 5 students
- Assigned membership of groups allows for the greatest personal growth
- The more variety in the group, the richer and better the result and the less potential for conflict.
- All groups must have a chairperson (this role should rotate amongst group members). Other group members may be assigned roles (recorder, checker, timekeeper, etc.).

4.3   Advantages and Disadvantages of Group Work

Advantages

- Learners actively involved
- Have learners work co-operatively, success depends on teamwork
- Learn respect for diverse talents and ways of learning

- Emphasize time spent on task, clear goals and expectations
- Provides prompt feedback on performance
- Overall better learning opportunity
- Opportunity to meet new people

4.3.1 Disadvantages

- Hard work!!
- Often appears unfair
- Involves **team** work, not just group work
- Good group work involves some risk taking e.g. 2 + 2 = 7

4.4 Basics of Interpersonal Skills

There are seven fundamental personal rights: The right ...
- to choose
- to have opinions
- to be respected
- to have needs
- to have and express feelings
- to make mistakes (and be forgiven)
- to accept these rights in others

There are also nine guidelines for conduct:

- We are all unique, show respect for each person as an individual
- Treat others the way you would like to be treated
- Look for good in others, expect the best
- If you don't have anything nice to say, don't say anything
- Be loyal first to yourself and then to others
- Maintain a sense of humour, keep things in perspective
- Cooperation must be earned, not demanded
- People don't care how much you know, just how much you care about them
- Show empathy

4.5 Feedback

To improve we need feedback. Learn how to respond to positive feedback, learn how to give constructive feedback to others.

- Focus feedback on a person's behaviour, not personality
- Focus on your observations rather than on inferences
- Sometimes you must take feedback with a grain of salt, you can't please all of the people all of the time

4.6   *How to be a Valuable Group Member*

- Attend to both task and morale components
- Do not fight for leadership - leadership rotates
- Help the chairperson be effective
- Help the group evolve, most groups do not start off great
- Assume the role(s) the group needs
- Reflect on each meeting
- Let others know of any complications

4.7   *How to be an Effective Chairperson*

- Anticipate the needs of the group, purpose of meeting, background issues, etc.
- Prepare the agenda. This is an important component of the chair's responsibility. An example of an agenda (say for a first meeting of the group) is as follows:
    a. Obtain names and phone numbers of group members
    b. List tasks or topics that might be worked on in the next week
    c. Identify the most important tasks
    d. Identify who will do which tasks
    e. Decide on time and place of next meeting
- Facilitate the meeting, be there ahead of time
- Seek feedback

4.8   *Coping with Conflict*

Conflict offers an opportunity to further develop the group. Learn different methods of coping with conflict. People are not difficult, their behaviours are!!

For the purpose of the assignments in this course, conflicts that cannot be resolved by the group should be brought to the attention of the TA or Instructor well before the assignment is due.

5.0 Research Skills

5.1 Introduction to Research Skills

Research skills are at the foundation of academic work. Students are often required to obtain information from different sources and compile the information for specific purposes. In upper year courses and higher level assignments, students may be asked to locate data through research and then compile this data into a meaningful summary. Sorting through the significant volumes of research available at the push of a button or in the library requires students to think clearly about their research goals and to critically evaluate sources of information to eliminate weaker sources.

5.2 Universal Intellectual Standards

Universal intellectual standards are standards which must be applied to thinking whenever one is interested in checking the quality of reasoning about a problem, issue, or situation. To think critically entails having command of these standards.

The standards are questions which probe the mind when assessing the quality of one's reasoning. The goal of these questions is to guide you to improving your reasoning skills.

The following is a quality of reasoning checklist:

1. **Clarity:** Could you elaborate further on that point? Could you express that point in another way? Could you give me an illustration? Could you give me an example? Clarity is the gateway standard. If a statement is unclear, we cannot determine whether it is accurate or relevant. In fact, we cannot tell anything about it because we do not yet know what it is saying. For example, the question, "What can be done about the education system in America?" is unclear. In order to address the question adequately, we would need to have a clearer understanding of what the person asking the question is considering the "problem" to be. A clearer question might be "What can educators do to ensure that students learn the skills and abilities which help them function successfully on the job and in their daily decision-making?"

2. **Accuracy:** Is that really true? How could we check that? How could we find out if that is true? A statement can be clear but not accurate, as in "Most dogs are over 300 pounds in weight."

3. **Precision:** Could you give more details? Could you be more specific? A statement can be both clear and accurate, but not precise, as in "Jack is overweight." (We do not know how overweight Jack is, one pound or 500 pounds.)

4. **Relevance:** How is that connected to the question? How does that bear on the issue? A statement can be clear, accurate, and precise, but not relevant to the question at hand. For example, students often think that the amount of effort they put into a course should be used in raising their grade in a course. Often, however, the "effort" does not measure the quality of student learning, and *when this is so*, effort is irrelevant to their appropriate grade.

5. **Depth:** How does your answer address the complexities in the question? How are you taking into account the problems in the question? Is that dealing with the most significant factors? A statement can be clear, accurate, precise, and relevant, but superficial (that is, lacking depth). For example, the statement "Just say No" which is often used to discourage children and teens from using drugs, is clear, accurate, precise, and relevant. Nevertheless, it lacks depth because it treats an extremely complex issue, the pervasive problem of drug use among young people, superficially. It fails to deal with the complexities of the issue.

6. **Breadth:** Do we need to consider another point of view? Is there another way to look at this question? What would this look like from a conservative standpoint? What would this look like from the point of view of ...? A line of reasoning may be clear, accurate, precise, relevant, and deep, but lack breadth (as in an argument from either the conservative or liberal standpoint which gets deeply into an issue, but only recognizes the insights of one side of the question.)

7. **Logic:** Does this really make sense? Does that follow from what you said? How does that follow? But before you implied this and now you are saying that; how can both be true? When we think, we bring a variety of thoughts together into some order. When the thoughts are mutually supporting and make sense in combination, the thinking is "logical." When the combination is not mutually supporting, is contradictory in some sense, or does not "make sense," the combination is not logical.

5.3   Guidelines for Critical Thinking

Critical thinking is an essential skill for any university student. Critical thinking is reasoned, reflective thinking that includes good judgment, is sensitive to the context, relies on identifiable criteria and is self correcting. Critical thinking skills require continued practice to develop. They are commonly used when reviewing arguments, reading reports, writing essays, reviewing of literature, and evaluating academic presentations. By developing critical thinking skills a student is better able to produce logical counter-arguments, identify weaknesses in an author's reasoning, identify misleading or inconsistent statements in literature, and present their own ideas, essays, and responses in an organized, coherent, and logical fashion.

When reviewing information it is important to address the following critical thinking questions:

- What is the main purpose and conclusion(s)?
- Is the purpose clearly and logically articulated?
- Are there any conflicts or assumptions present in the reasoning?

- Do fallacies exist in the reasoning?
- Do alternative ways to solve the problem exist?
- Are the alternatives a better option?
- Is the evidence used to support the argument credible and accurate?
- Has any significant information been omitted or manipulated?
- Have all possible conclusions been evaluated from the arguments presented?

Whether writing or reading an essay, an individual utilizing critical thinking skills will be more capable to gather all relevant information, note inconsistencies or errors in the information, and then respond with an educated rebuttal. Learning and perfecting critical thinking skills will provide a student with an academic advantage.

5.4   Evaluating Websites

A website evaluation assesses the integrity of a website by considering components such as scope, evidence, validity, etc. Each component is ranked on a scale of 0 through 5; 0 being the lowest and 5 being the highest. If the website receives a score between 75-100%, then it is considered a reliable website.

A reliable website is necessary when conducting scientific research as the World Wide Web can be utilized and accessed by anyone. Furthermore, online documents do not require any editing or monitoring. Therefore, it becomes the job of the researcher to assess any information in an educated and critical manner to ensure that the acquired information is accurate.

QUESTIONS TO KEEP IN MIND WHILE EVALUATING WEBSITE MATERIAL	RANK
SCOPE: How valuable and important is the information in the site relative to other material on the same subject at other websites? Low score for lack of content, obvious omissions etc.	
EVIDENCE: Is there evidence to support the author's claims? Is the evidence convincing or believable? What is the quality of the information? Low score for lack of evidence or poor evidence to support claims.	
VALIDITY: How accurate are the "facts" on the website? Can you verify that the information is correct? Has the information been peer-reviewed? Low score for inaccuracies, misquoting etc.	
AUTHOR: Can you find out who sent/wrote the information? Can you verify whether the author is an authority or expert in the field of the information they are publishing? (ie. what are the author's credentials, professional background/experience etc.?) Is there a way to contact the author, e-mail or phone? Low score for missing name of author, contact info, or if author is not qualified to write on that subject matter.	
SPONSORSHIP: Did a professional body or educational institute sponsor/fund the site? Do they have a vested interest in the subject matter? (ie. a pharmaceutical company marketing its product, advocacy group trying to rally up supporters etc.) Low score for biased material, ulterior motives, lack of objectivity and so forth.	
BALANCE: Is the information biased? Does the author present pro and con arguments equally and fairly? Low score for biased material, ulterior motives, lack of objectivity etc.	

REFERENCES: Does the author reference other material, internet or hard copy articles that can be checked for verification or clarification? Are there hyperlinks to other websites? Low score for absence of references or incorrectly cited references.	
DATEDNESS: When was the information published or posted? Has it been updated recently? How recent is the information? Low score for out-of-date material.	
NAVIGATION/DESIGN: How well organized was the information? How easy was it to navigate around the website? Were there logical sections and subsections? Was there an internal index or table of contents? Low score for difficulty in navigating, finding index, hyperlinks etc.	

5.5 Writing a Thesis Statement

Writing in university often requires that you convince or persuade your reader that your interpretation or understanding of a topic is correct. The way to do this in an academic paper is to decide on a topic and after a brief introduction, state your point of view on the topic directly and often in one sentence. This sentence is the thesis statement, and it serves as a summary of the argument you'll make in the rest of your paper.

A thesis statement:

- Tells the reader how you will interpret the significance of the subject matter under discussion.
- Is a road map for the paper; in other words, it tells the reader what to expect from the rest of the paper.
- Directly answers the question asked of you. A thesis is an interpretation of a question or subject, not the subject itself. The subject, or topic, of a paper might be ground water contamination; a thesis must then offer a way to understand the subject.
- Makes a claim that others might dispute.
- Is usually a single sentence somewhere in your first paragraph that presents your argument to the reader. The rest of the paper, the body, gathers and organizes evidence that will persuade the reader of the logic of your interpretation.

5.5.1 Tips for Writing Your Thesis Statement

1. Determine what kind of paper you are writing:

   - An **analytical** paper breaks down an issue or an idea into its component parts, evaluates the issue or idea, and presents this breakdown and evaluation to the audience.
   - An **expository** (explanatory) paper explains something to the audience.
   - An **argumentative** paper makes a claim about a topic and justifies this claim with specific evidence. The claim could be an opinion, a policy proposal, an evaluation, a cause-and-effect statement, or an interpretation. The goal of the argumentative paper is to convince the audience that the claim is true based on the evidence provided.

2. Your thesis statement should be specific—it should cover only what you will discuss in your paper and should be supported with specific evidence.

3. The thesis statement usually appears at the end of the first paragraph of a paper.

4. Your topic may change as you write, so you may need to revise your thesis statement to reflect exactly what you have discussed in the paper.

5.5.2   *Some Myths about Thesis Statements*

- *A thesis statement must come at the end of the first paragraph.* This is a natural position for a statement of focus, but it's not the only one. Some theses can be stated in the opening sentences of a paper; others need a paragraph or two of introduction; others can't be fully formulated until the end.
- *A thesis statement must be one sentence in length, no matter how many clauses it contains.* Clear writing is more important than rules like these. Use two or three sentences if you need them. A complex argument may require a whole tightly-knit paragraph to make its initial statement of position.
- *You can't start writing a paper until you have a perfect thesis statement.* It may be advisable to draft a hypothesis or tentative thesis statement near the start of a big project, but changing and refining a thesis is a main task of thinking your way through your ideas as you write a paper. And some papers need to explore the question in depth without being locked in before they can provide even a tentative answer.
- *A thesis statement must give three points of support.* It should indicate that the paper will explain and give evidence for its assertion, but points don't need to come in any specific number.

6.0   Fieldwork & Methods

6.1   Introduction to Fieldwork

Fieldwork is an important part of the Geography program at McMaster University. Fieldwork provides students with hands on, real world learning experiences. In SGES programs students learn proper field methods. A variety of different field experiences are available to students both within individual courses and as entire courses.

While fieldwork can be exciting, there can also be situations which are dangerous. It is important to take the time to learn about proper safety procedures and equipment for each field situation and be aware of safety while in the field. Some situations can be demanding and may require good physical fitness and some endurance to successfully complete a project. A good pair of shoes or boots are recommended for fieldwork.

This chapter will introduce the basics of fieldwork, including taking field notes.

6.2   Field Notes (Observations & Sketch Maps)

Field notes are written records of fieldwork, made at the time the work is done. They provide descriptive information to accompany the collected data. Field notes must be as complete and as accurate as possible, because the most careful and reliable fieldwork will be of little or no value if the record of the work is unreliable. The collection of good field notes is as important as any other task involved in fieldwork and it often proves to be the most difficult; requiring alertness, care, accuracy and intelligence.

Essential items to bring along:
a hard pencil (HB)
eraser
field notebook (preferably with a hard cover)
ruler (straight edge)
graph paper
camera (optional)

6.2.1   How to take good field notes:

1. Use a hard pencil (HB) and keep it sharp; never use ink.
2. Hand-write (print) notes, making them clear enough to be read by someone else. Typed notes are not acceptable.
3. Do not trust anything to memory; if in doubt, write it down.
4. Label the top of each page with a short descriptive title so that one can tell at a glance what the notes on that page are about.
5. The date should appear at the top of each page.

6. Describe categorical data: the date, the location, the weather, the time of day, the season, etc.
7. Make sketches or take photographs to record important visual observations.
8. Review field notes at the end of each day and add any missing information.
9. Do not rewrite notes after the fieldwork, as this can lead to the introduction of analytical components rather than pure observations.

6.2.2 Essential Components of Field Notes:

- **Observations**: categorical information, natural and built environments, social behaviour, and categorical observations.
- **Sketch Maps:** physical and built (human) landscape, human activity, etc.

6.2.2.1 Observations

In your observations you record what you see and make sense of what is important. This is a skill to be developed through practice. To simplify the process, observational notes are generally organized into three types; categorical, physical space (built environment); and human or social activity. Details about each of these types are provided below. In general, you need to consider being as precise as you can, but avoid getting bogged down in the details; making generalizations is an important part of doing research.

Categorical Observations:
- What? Where? When?

Observations of the Built Environment:
- Observe the natural and built environments
- How is space organized? What is the physical layout of the space?
- What features are apparent?
- What materials are used?

Observations of the Social Environment:
- Observe how space is being used (or not used)
- What is the level of social interaction?
- Observe how the natural and built environment influences human behaviour, and aides or impedes human movement

Typically, researchers also include a fourth component in their observations that they make while in the field. This fourth component of observations is called reflections. Reflections include one's initial thoughts to explain what is being observed.

Observational Reflections:
- Why is space used (or not used)?
- Why is space organized as it is?
- What influence does the organization of space have on its use?

Below is an example of a set of observational notes (not including reflections). Note that the observations are hand-written, and are organized using the categorical, built environment, and social environment nomenclature.

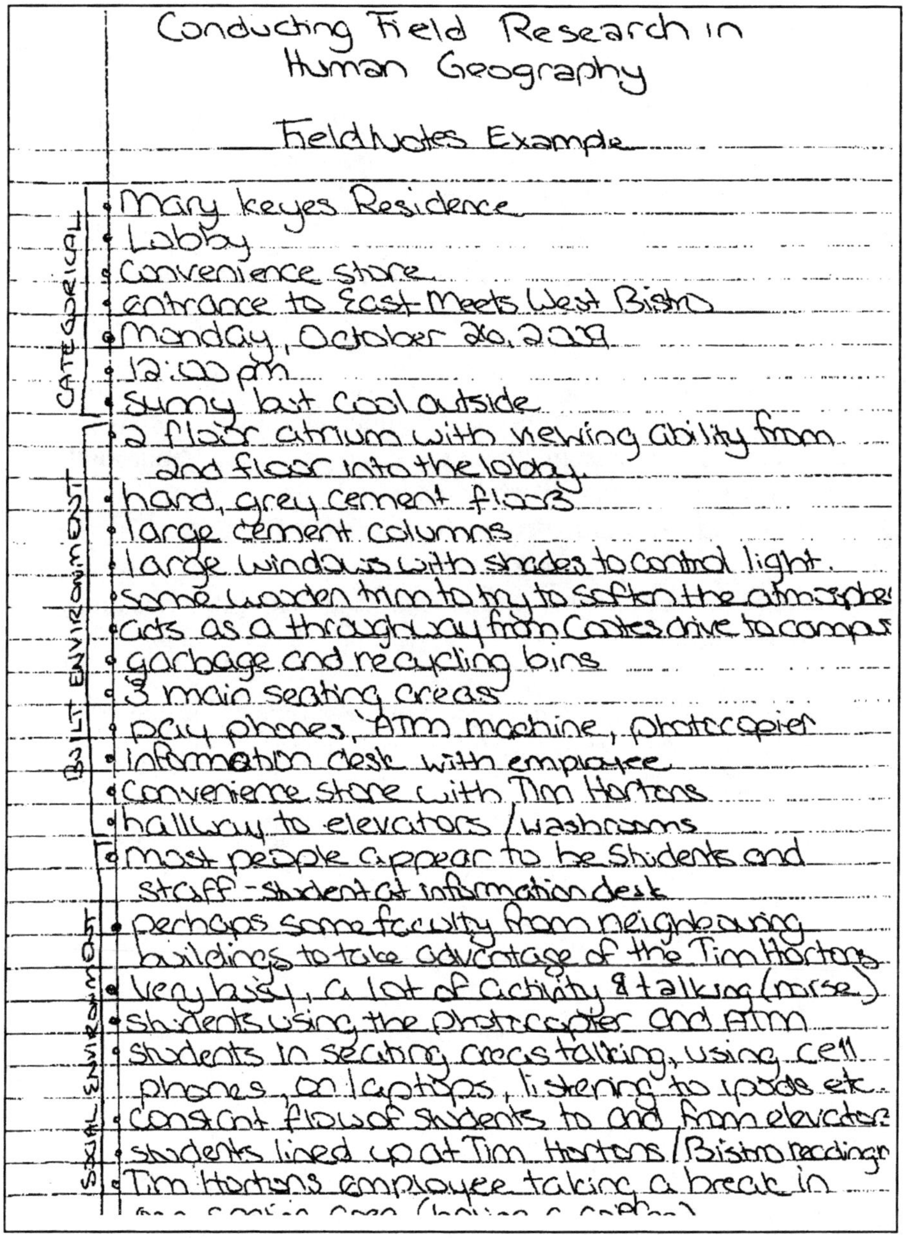

Conducting Field Research in
Human Geography

Field Notes Example

CATEGORICAL
- Mary Keyes Residence
- Lobby
- Convenience store
- entrance to East Meets West Bistro
- Monday, October 26, 2009
- 12:00 pm
- Sunny but cool outside

BUILT ENVIRONMENT
- 2 floor atrium with viewing ability from 2nd floor into the lobby.
- hard, grey cement floors
- large cement columns
- large windows with shades to control light.
- some wooden trim to try to soften the atmosphere
- acts as a throughway from Cootes drive to campus
- garbage and recycling bins
- 3 main seating areas
- pay phones, ATM machine, photocopier
- information desk with employee
- Convenience store with Tim Hortons.
- hallway to elevators / washrooms

SOCIAL ENVIRONMENT
- most people appear to be students and staff - student at information desk
- perhaps some faculty from neighbouring buildings to take advantage of the Tim Hortons
- Very busy, a lot of activity & talking (noise)
- students using the photocopier and ATM
- students in seating areas talking, using cell phones, on laptops, listening to ipods etc.
- constant flow of students to and from elevator
- students lined up at Tim Hortons / Bistro reading
- Tim Hortons employee taking a break in the seating area (having a coffee)

Figure 6.1: Observational Field Notes of the Lobby of Mary Keyes Residence, McMaster.

6.2.2.2   Sketch Maps

When performing fieldwork, it is always a good idea to draw a sketch map of the field site. A sketch map should contain all of the pertinent information for the site. Sketch maps are a key component of field notes, and are a visual reflection of much of what is in your observations.

Sketch maps should be as large as possible with clear annotations so they may be easily interpreted by someone who is not familiar with geographic maps.   All sketch maps should include the following information:

- title
- north arrow
- boundary (a box outlining your map)
- scale
- clear labels and annotation of the features shown
- boundary lines should be drawn with a straight edge
- a legend (if needed)
- to clarify a portion of the map, draw it in a larger scale beside the main map (this is called an inset map)

The level of detail recorded on a sketch map will vary depending on the scale of the site being studied. The types of features, for example, that might influence human activity will vary depending on whether you are considering one room in a building or an entire neighbourhood. For example, consider a room on campus; if someone placed a table right in the middle of the room, this would impede traffic flow, would encourage people to put things on it, etc. The placement of this table would have a relatively significant influence on the human activity in that room. That same table, placed in the middle of campus would have little to no influence on the human activity patterns of the entire campus.

The point is, the types of things that are important to note in your observations, or on a sketch map, will vary depending on the scale of the site being examined. Below are two examples of sketch maps, each for a different scale of site.

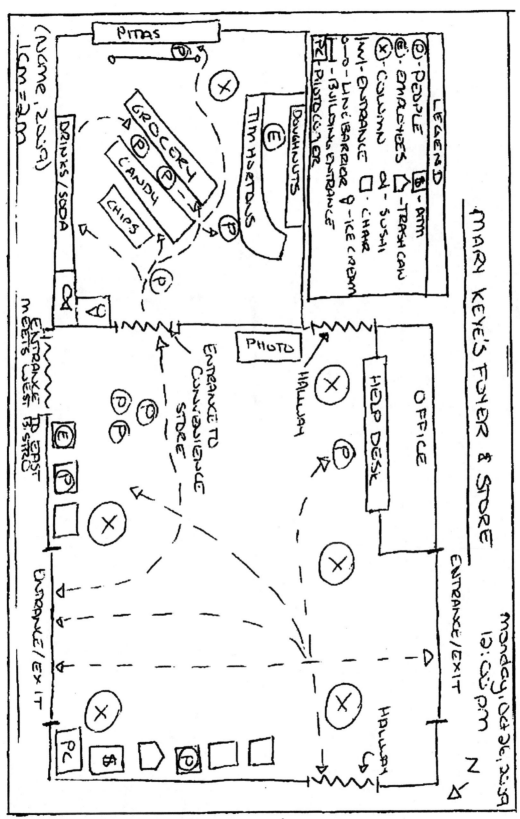

Figure 6.2: Sketch Map of Lobby of Mary Keyes Residence, McMaster

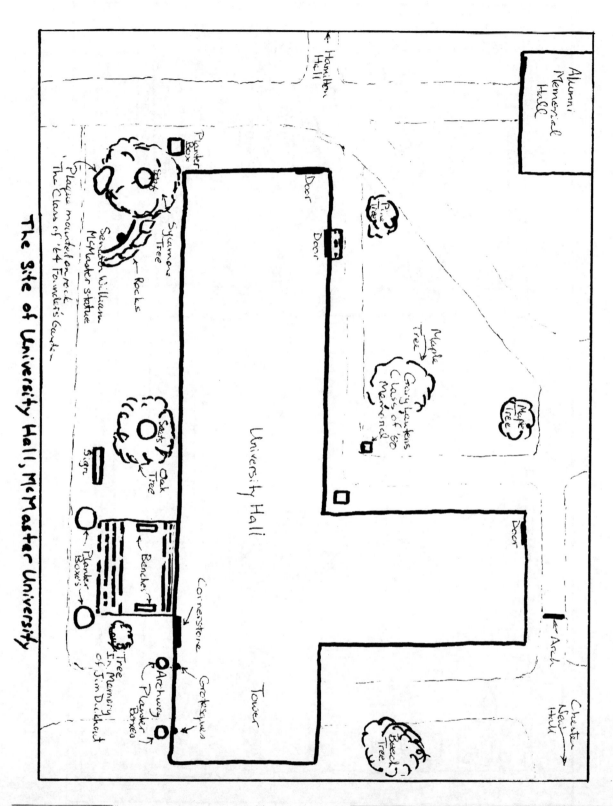

Figure 6.3: Sketch Map of the Site of University Hall, McMaster.

6.2.3 Supplemental/Optional Components of Field Notes:

- **Sketches** (where necessary): outlines, profiles of buildings, relative locations, and topographical features, as needed to describe the recorded data.
- **Explanatory notes** (where necessary): notes which help to clarify both sketches and observations.
- **Photographs** (where necessary): a permanent record of the research site which can clarify field notes at a later date.

6.2.3.1 Sketches

In general, if measurements cannot be easily described, or if the written description of a series of measurements would take more time or space than a simple sketch, make a sketch. **Always** make a sketch when it will settle any questions which might arise in the interpretation of the notes, or if it will assist in readily understanding the work done.

- Make sketches large, open and clear. Use the right-hand pages of the notebook when possible, but it is not necessary to leave the opposite pages blank, they may be used as well.
- Sketches may be drawn free-hand. However, it is a better idea to use a straight edge for lines.
- The protractor is seldom used in the field; angles are usually estimated by sight. In some instances one may purposely exaggerate angles in order to clarify their meaning.
- Portions of a sketch drawn to a larger scale are often needed and should be located either towards one side of the main sketch, or on another page.
- Sketches should be fully annotated.
- It can be very useful to take a photograph of the region or part of the region being sketched.

6.2.3.2 Explanatory Notes

The object of these notes is to clarify anything which is not perfectly evident from the measurements or sketches, and to provide a record of information concerning important features of the survey area and the work done for later use.

- Place the notes in vacant spaces where they will not interfere with recorded measurements, dimension lines, or sketches. Be as BRIEF and CONCISE as possible.
- Use explanatory notes if the recorded dimensions or sketches need an oral explanation, should someone else use the notes. The resulting notes should contain sufficient information to enable another individual to make a complete plan of your survey from the notebook alone.
- Review your notes each evening and augment with any missing details

6.2.3.3   *Photographs*

- Establish a numbering system to identify photographs and maintain this within in your field notes.

- Record the date and time of all photographs taken to ensure that they can be easily identified.

- In every photo include some familiar object (e.g., hammer, ruler, person, etc.) to incorporate a scale into the photo. It is very easy to take a picture of a small feature such as a ripple and later identify it in a photo as a dune.

- If printed, place some type of identification on all photos before they get out of sequence.

- With the advent of digital cameras, you can take additional images at no additional cost. This allows you to take many images which may be useful when later interpreting your field notes.

> Remember to keep a log of each photo you take with a numbering system.
> It is not always easy to identify pictures, especially if it takes a while
> to get them labelled on a computer or get them processed.

6.3   *Fieldwork in an Urban Setting:*

Here are some suggestions for conducting fieldwork in an urban setting:

1. Safety: Always work with a partner (or partners). Most field exercises you will be asked to do in geography will require you to work as part of a group. You should always conduct your fieldwork during daytime hours.

2. Etiquette: Always respect the privacy and property rights of others. Remember that you are representing both McMaster University and the School of Geography & Earth Sciences (in addition to yourself and your Instructor), so you are expected to be professional and respectful of others.

3. Timing: Be sure to conduct your fieldwork as soon as possible after it is assigned. This will ensure that you have time to return to the field site at a later date (if necessary). This will also reduce the probability of having to conduct your fieldwork in inclement weather.

4. Requirements: The following should be considered necessities for doing fieldwork: hardcover notebook, hard (HB) pencil for writing field notes and making sketches, and a camera.

5. Field Notes: Be sure to make your field notes while you are in the field (hence the

notebook, pencil, etc.). Your notes are likely to be both incomplete and inaccurate if you write them up in the comfort of your home.

6. Reflection: It is often good practice to supplement your field notes, upon your return from the field, with some post-fieldwork reflections. Consider your fieldwork, and think about what you observed, and what it means. Add these notes as an appendix to your true field notes.

7.0   Topographic Maps

7.1   Origin of Topographic Maps

In 1927, the Federal Government introduced a single system of maps based on an orderly progression of scales and a single set of specifications. Prior to this time civilian and military agencies worked independently and produced useful maps at a variety of scales. The problem was the lack of continuity between maps.

Location of Topographic Maps at McMaster University
A complete set of Canadian topographic maps can be accessed in the Lloyd Reeds Map Library located within Mills Library. Many US and International maps are located here as well.
The library has over 125 000 maps as well as up to date digital data.

Modern topographic maps are produced by aerial photography and the global positioning system (GPS). The GPS is a series of satellites that emit continuous signals. A receiver on the ground can interpret the exact position of the satellite as well as the distance from the satellite to the receiver at that point in time. A computer built into the receiver can read signals from several passing satellites and compute its exact position on the Earth's system. The GPS can also be useful in determining elevations on the Earth's surface within one metre.

7.2   Topographic Map Content

Topographic maps contain a vast amount of information regarding the location of a particular region on the Earth's surface, its physical features, vegetation, and human (or cultural) characteristics. This information is presented on a map through the use of standardized labels, symbols, colours and lines.

7.2.1.1   Information provided on the map border

A large amount of information is presented on the borders of a topographic map sheet. This information includes:
   a) the publishing information (where, when and by whom the map was published,)
   b) a partial legend (a complete legend is found on the back of the map sheet).
   c) a title
   d) a graphic scale
   e) an elevation conversion scale (converting imperial units to metric units)
   f) a statement of the contour interval (e.g. 10m)
   g) edition and map sheet information
   h) an index to adjoining topographic maps
   i) an example to calculate grid reference
   j) a statement of the magnetic declination of the sheet

Figure 7.1 shows where the information listed above is found on the borders of a topographic map.

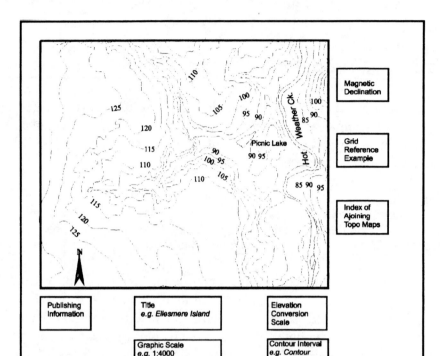

Figure 7.1: The location of information on the borders of a topographic map

7.3   *Contour Lines*

Topographic maps are two-dimensional, scaled down representations of the Earth's three-dimensional surface. In order to represent the three-dimensional shape of the Earth's surface, topographic maps use contour lines to represent height (or elevation) of various geographical features. A contour line connects all points on the map that have the same elevation above sea level. The '0m' contour represents sea level. Contour lines are important because they are an effective method of depicting the topography (configuration) of the land surface on a map. By noting the arrangement, spacing and changing shapes of contour lines, the map reader can obtain a remarkably accurate concept of the 'lay of the land' or topography of the area represented by the map. The following example illustrates how contours are drawn to represent topography on a map.

Example:
To construct the topographic map representing the island shown in Figure 7.2, the following steps are taken:
1.   A 0-metre contour line is drawn at sea level (A).
2.   Contour lines are drawn where any plane of elevation (such as B or C) intersects the surface of the island. A 50-metre contour line is drawn to represent the plane

of 50 metres above sea level (B). A 100-metre contour line is drawn to represent the plane of 100 metres above sea level (C).

3. The topographic map shown in D is drawn using a 50m contour interval.

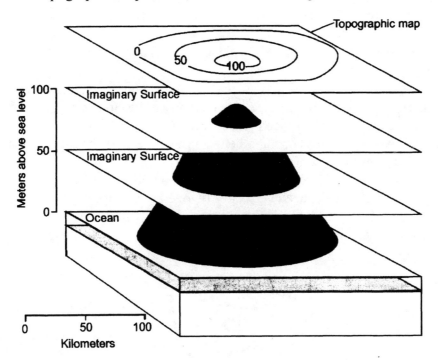

Figure 7.2: How to construct contours on a topographic map

Contours are also drawn by interpolating between the known elevations of well marked features such as the summits of hills, points along railway lines or roads, dams, and the floors of valleys. These points of known elevation are called spot heights. Figure 7.3 shows the construction of a contour line from points of known elevation.

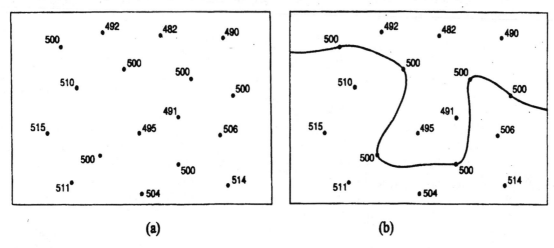

Figure 7.3: Construction of a contour line: (a) points of known elevation, (b) the same points with a 500-metre contour line added.

7.3.1 Rules for the interpretation of contour lines:

There are a number of 'rules' that must be followed when interpreting surface topography based on contour lines. The following is a handy reference for these rules.

1. Contour lines connect points of equal elevation. Thus, every point along a contour line is at the exact same elevation.
2. Contour lines are always closed. Occasionally a contour line extends beyond the boundary of the map. In this case you cannot see the closure as the contour line stops at the map boundary (see Figure 7.3b above).
3. Contour lines never cross one another except where an overhanging cliff exists. In this case the 'hidden' contours are dashed.
4. Contour lines that are evenly spaced represent a uniform slope.
5. Contour lines that are spaced very closely together represent a steep slope, whereas widely spaced contour lines indicate a more gradual slope.
6. Contour lines that form a series of concentric circles represent a hill.

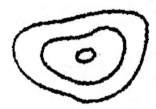

7. Contour lines that represent a depression are shown by a series of concentric circles with hachure marks on the downhill side.

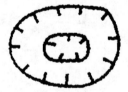

8. Contour lines that cross a stream form a 'V pattern'. The apex of the 'V' points to higher elevation (i.e. upstream).

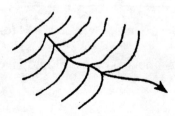

7.4   Map Scales

A topographic map uses a small piece of paper to portray the complex form of part of the Earth's surface that may cover many square kilometres. As a result, the map must show features at a different scale to those actually present on the ground. The map **scale** represents the relationship between the measured distance between objects on the ground and the distance shown on the map sheet.

7.4.1   Type of Scale:

7.4.1.1   Representative Fraction

The most common method used to identify scale on topographic maps is the representative fraction such as 1:10,000 (1/10,000). This means that one unit on the map represents 10,000 units on the Earth's surface. For example, 1 cm on the map would represent 10,000 cm or 100 m on the ground. The properties of the representative fraction are always constant:

- the numerator is always 1.
- the numerator always represents the distance on the map.
- the denominator always represents the distance on the Earth's surface.
- the numerator and denominator always represent the same units of measurement.

7.4.1.2   Graphic Scale

The graphic scale consists of a short line divided into a number of smaller units, each of which represents a distance on the Earth's surface. To use this scale to find actual distances, the distance between points is measured on the map and the corresponding distance is read off the graphic scale.

For example:
The distance from point A to B measured on the map in Figure 7.4 is 4.4 cm which corresponds to 4.4 km on the graphic scale. Therefore, the distance on the Earth's surface from point A to B is 4.4 km.

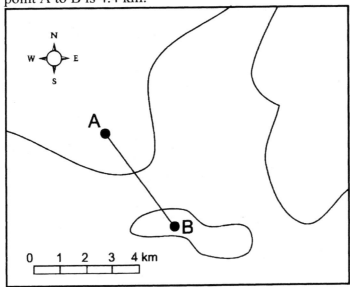

Figure 7.4: A simple map illustrating the use of a graphic scale.

153

7.4.1.3   *Verbal Scale*

The verbal scale describes the relationship between the map and real world distance in written form, e.g. 1 cm represents 1 km. Note that the word "represents" is used to describe the relationship. Expressions such as 1 cm "equals" 1 km are invalid and must not be used.

7.5   Grid References

It is important that the location of features shown on a topographic map can be communicated to others. Geographical coordinates (latitude and longitude) are imprecise at the scale of most topographic map features, and a grid system is superimposed over the map sheet. The grid system is composed of vertical (Easting) and horizontal (Northing) lines where each line has a 2 digit numerical value. Any feature on a topographic map can be located by reference to this grid system.

A grid reference has six figures separated into two components. The first three figures are the "Easting" component (the X coordinate) and the last three figures are the "Northing" component (the Y coordinate). No comma is used to separate the two parts.

Grid references are determined as follows:
(i)   Find the Easting component by using the grid line immediately west (left of the feature in question) as the first two digits. Then estimate the number of tenths the feature is towards the grid line to the east. This number is the third digit of the Easting coordinate.
(ii)   Find the Northing component in a similar manner; by taking the grid line south (below) the feature as the first two digits and estimating tenths to the north (upwards) to obtain the third.
(iii)   Place the Easting component in front of the Northing component to complete the 6 figure grid reference.

For example, the grid reference for the dot shown on the map in Figure 7.5 is 310884.

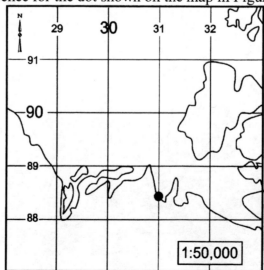

Figure 7.5: A simple map with grid lines.

154

7.6　*Human Geography Features*

In addition to documenting the natural landscape, topographic maps are an excellent tool for documenting the human use of land. A series of standardized symbols have been developed to depict various human activities such as homes and other buildings, recreational facilities, institutions such as schools, churches, etc. Below are a series of examples of some of these symbols.

7.6.1　*Recreational Features:*

Feature Name	Symbol
Sports track	
Swimming pool	
Stadium	
Golf course	
Golf driving range	
Campground; Picnic site	
Ski area, ski jump	
Rifle range with butts	
Historic site or point of interest; Navigation light	
Aerial cableway, ski lift	

7.6.2　*Other Man-Made Features (e.g. buildings, etc.):*

Feature Name	Symbol
School; Fire station; Police station	
Church; Non-Christian place of worship; Shrine	
Building	
Service centre	
Customs post	

Coast Guard station	.ⓒ
Cemetery	C
Ruins	R
Fort	

Source: Natural Resources Canada - http://maps.nrcan.gc.ca/topo101/symbols_e.php

8.0   References

Bourne, L., & Ley, D. (Eds.) (1993). *The changing social geography of Canadian cities.* Montreal: McGill-Queen's University Press.

Environment Canada. (1966). *The state of Canada's environment.* Ottawa: Queen's Printer.

Geological Survey of Canada. (2004, February). *A map of Canada's earth materials.* Retrieved December 1, 2006, from http://canada.geoscape.nrcan.gc.ca/geo_can_t2/index_e.aspx.

Goldschneider, F., Waite, L., & Witsberger, C. (1986). Nonfamily living and the erosion of traditional family orientations among young adults. *American Sociological Review, 51*, 541-554.

Harris, R. (1996). *Unplanned suburbs: Toronto's American tragedy.* Baltimore: Johns Hopkins University Press.

Johnson, J. (2009). Plugging into the sun. *National Geographic, Sept.* 28-53.

Knox, P., & Pinch, S. (2006). *Urban social geography: An introduction.* Toronto: Pearson-Prentice Hall.

Kuby, M., Harner, J., & Gober, P. (2007). *Human geography in action.* Hoboken, NJ: John Wiley & Sons.

Lewis, R. (2001). A city transformed: Manufacturing districts and suburban growth in Montreal, 1850-1941. *Journal of Historical Geography, 27*, 20-35.

Mercier, Michael. (2010). The geography of language. GEOG 1HA3, McMaster University, November 30.

Moore, E. & Rosenberg, M. (1993). Migration, mobility and population redistribution. In L. Bourne & D. Ley (Eds.) *The changing social geography of Canadian cities* (pp. 121-137). Montreal: McGill-Queen's University Press.

Northey, M., D. Draper & Knight, D. (2015). *Making sense: A student's guide to research and writing in geography and the environmental sciences.* (6th ed.). Toronto: Oxford University Press.

Norton, W. (2009). *Human geography* (7th ed.). Toronto: Oxford University Press.

Shaffer, R. (1983). Digital audio already altering recording industry's practices. *The Wall Street Journal, April 29*, 27.